Battle of Britain
The Movie

Battle of Britain
The Movie

The Men and Machines of one of the Greatest War Films Ever Made

Robert J. Rudhall and
Dilip Sarkar MBE, FRHistS

First published in Great Britain in 2000 by Ramrod Books.
This revised and updated edition published in 2023 and reprinted in 2025 by
Air World
An imprint of
Pen & Sword Books Ltd
Yorkshire – Philadelphia

Copyright © Estate of Robert J. Rudhall,
and Dilip Sarkar MBE, FRHistS, 2023

HB ISBN 978 1 39901 475 5
PB ISBN 978 1 39901 479 3

The right of Robert J. Rudhall and Dilip Sarkar MBE, FRHistS to be identified as the Authors of this work has been asserted by them in accordance with the Copyright, Designs and Patents Act 1988. A CIP catalogue record for this book is available from the British Library All rights reserved.

No part of this book may be reproduced or transmitted in any form or by any means, electronic or mechanical including photocopying, recording or by any information storage and retrieval system, without permission from the Publisher in writing.

Typeset by Mac Style
Printed in the UK by CPI Group (UK) Ltd, Croydon, CR0 4YY.

Pen & Sword Books Limited incorporates the imprints of After the Battle, Archaeology, Atlas, Aviation, Discovery, Family History, Fiction, History, Maritime, Military, Military Classics, Politics, Select, Transport, True Crime, Air World, Frontline Publishing, Leo Cooper, Remember When, Seaforth Publishing, The Praetorian Press, Wharncliffe Local History, Wharncliffe Transport, Wharncliffe True Crime and White Owl

For a complete list of Pen & Sword titles please contact:

PEN & SWORD BOOKS LTD
47 Church Street, Barnsley, South Yorkshire, S70 2AS, UK.
E-mail: enquiries@pen-and-sword.co.uk
Website: www.pen-and-sword.co.uk

or

PEN AND SWORD BOOKS,
1950 Lawrence Road, Havertown, PA 19083, USA
E-mail: Uspen-and-sword@casematepublishers.com
Website: www.penandswordbooks.com

This book is dedicated in memory of Robert Rudhall – and to his widow, Joyce, for her unfailing love and support of Robert on this project and beyond

The sadly late Robert Rudhall and Dilip Sarkar and the launch of their original *Battle of Britain: The Movie*, and the latter's *Battle of Britain: The Photographic Kaleidoscope, Volume II*, Worcester Guildhall, May 2000.

Contents

Foreword to the New Edition		viii
Reel 1	Introduction to the Original Edition	1
Reel 2	Opening Shots	4
Reel 3	Film Logistics	23
Reel 4	Lights, Cameras, Action!	30
Reel 5	Battle's Camera Ship	40
Reel 6	Colours and Codes	46
Reel 7	Model Work	52
Reel 8	On Location	57
Reel 9	Summer 1968	68
Reel 10	Identifying the Royal Air Force	102
Reel 11	Music Maketh the Movie	109
Reel 12	On Release	125
Reel 13	Cast and Credits	134
Reel 14	The Aircraft Fleet, Then and Now	151
Reel 15	The Big and 'Fantastic' Story: Battle of Britain in Context	164
Appendix I: 1969 – A Year in Film and Television		212
Appendix II: Battle of Britain 'Stars' Filmography		214
Appendix III: Also Seen In …		217
Acknowledgements		218
Bibliography		220

Foreword to the New Edition

In 1969, *Battle of Britain* was released and over half a century later remains the greatest aviation war film ever made – the greatest war film ever made, in the opinion of many. The film inspired, in fact, a whole new wave of interest in the Battle of Britain period, the vintage aircraft assembled for the flying sequences igniting the modern warbird movement. Moreover, a whole new generation subsequently became fascinated by the subject, researching the men and machines of the actual battle, leading to a plethora of amateur enthusiast groups and museums dedicated to telling this epic story. The legacy of *Battle of Britain*, therefore, goes far beyond whatever it achieved at the box office or through film critics' reviews – and how many films could lay claim to having had such a lasting impact?

Amongst those who fell under the magical appeal of *Battle of Britain* was the sadly now late Robert Rudhall. A Herefordian, Robert later settled in Tewkesbury, Gloucestershire, where his father was Chief Projectionist at the local cinema – hence Robert's early interest in movies. Although working full-time in the aviation industry, having been trained by his father, Robert also worked as a part-time projectionist, sound and lighting technician at the town's Roses Theatre – meeting some of the great names in variety and theatre.

Robert's passion for aviation was inspired by 1960s airshows at Staverton, Gloucester, where he was later heavily involved with the Skyfame Aircraft Museum. In 1979, he was a founder member of the Cotswold Aircraft Restoration Group and, having contributed articles to the aviation press for many years, in 1991 became Assistant Editor of the popular *FlyPast* magazine.

Having already been hooked on war films, comics and models, I couldn't personally say that that *Battle of Britain* alone inspired my own interest – but it certainly cemented it and helped draw me into what could be described as an obsession with the events of summer 1940. My first book was published in 1990, and two years later I set up my own specialist

Foreword to the New Edition   ix

publishing company, Ramrod Publications, which Robert approached in 1999, inquiring whether we would be interested in publishing his first book, *Battle of Britain: The Movie*. The answer was a resounding 'Yes!' without having even seen the material. Although up to that point I had not met Robert personally, I knew of him by reputation as a hugely knowledgeable and decent chap, who was highly respected and well-liked – and easy to work with. When I did see his draft, I was not disappointed: the text and photographs were everything I had every confidence they would be.

We launched the book at Worcester Guildhall in May 2000, alongside my *Battle of Britain: The Photographic Kaleidoscope Volume II*. Various personalities connected with the making of the film joined us, including the composer Ron Goodwin, and, as usual, many of the Few, including Air Chief Marshal Sir Christopher Foxley-Norris and Air Commodore Peter Brothers, respectively Chairman and Deputy Chairman of the exulted Battle of Britain Fighter Association. Other guests included The Hon. Lady Odette Dowding and Lady Bader, and for Robert the day was one at times, before he came to us, he thought would never come, having, astonishingly, been rejected by other publishers. That afternoon, we were treated to Lancaster PA474 of the Battle of Britain Memorial Flight roaring over Worcester High Street and the Guildhall. A brilliant day and a great launch. The book soon sold out, in fact, leading to another batch being produced, and Robert and I enjoyed various signing sessions together at IWM Duxford and Biggin Hill. Good times, happy days, great memories. The following year we produced Robert's Battle of Britain Film: The Photo Album, which was similarly successful, and, I believe, both books did the film and enthusiasts a great service, given the lack of up-to-date material on the subject available at that time.

Tragically, in 2003, Robert died suddenly, aged 52, leaving behind his devoted best friend and widow, Joyce. Robert's loss was keenly felt by the aviation historical community. It was an appropriate mark of respect, and an indication of this incredibly talented, kind and modest man's popularity, that his ashes were scattered from PA474, in which Robert had flown, over the IWM Duxford airfield - where a memorial service was subsequently held.

This new edition is very much a tribute to Robert, who remains much-missed: RIP, old friend.

Dilip Sarkar MBE, FRHistS, 2021

Reel 1

Introduction to the Original Edition

Why write a book about a film which was premiered over 30 years ago? That is a question I have been asked many times over the past few years. My answer has always been, surely the film deserves it! After all, several vintage aircraft owe their current existence to this feature film. While it may not have made much, or any, money at the box office, the historic aircraft movement throughout the world would be much the poorer today had it not been for Messrs Fisz and Saltzman's endeavours to re-create for the silver screen one of the most crucial periods of Britain's history.

Back in 1940 this country stood alone, and why it fought to beat off the Nazi invader has been well documented in many books on the subject

Replica Hurricanes awaiting the 'strafing attack' by 'Me 109s' on their 'French airfield' at Duxford, 1968. (*Peter Arnold Collection* [*PAC*])

2 Battle of Britain: The Movie

Not since the Second World War had so many Hurricanes and Spitfires gathered together – Henlow, April 1968. (*PAC*)

over the years. *Battle of Britain* was the first major film to deal with the aerial conflicts above Britain during 1940 in its entirety. Previous films had looked at certain areas of the Battle or at some of the personalities, but the whole story of the epic struggle of 1940 had not been tackled by the film industry until Saltzman and Fisz came along.

Leonard Mosley's book on the making of the film, published by *Weidenfeld & Nicolson* in 1969 is still looked on by many, including myself, as 'the bible' when it comes to the film's production. While I do not attempt to imitate this much thumbed tome, my effort seeks to deal more with the aircraft hardware, the locations and to give it deserved credit for the effect it had on the preservation of old aircraft in the UK, and indeed, worldwide.

I can vividly remember going to see *Battle of Britain* at the Odeon, New Street, Birmingham, on 2 October 1969, just a couple of weeks after it was premiered. I gazed in wonderment at the impressive foyer display, where a whole host of large-scale models were suspended from the ceiling in mock dogfights. A sales area in one corner was selling copies of Mosley's aforementioned book, a souvenir programme of the film, the long-playing soundtrack record (no CDs in those days) and a set of 32 colour postcards, complete with boxed album (I still have in my possession all of these now much treasured items).

On entering the cinema's lavish auditorium, the screen curtains were bathed in the red, white and blue colours of the Royal Air Force, giving the feeling that what was to come was something special. Before long the lights dimmed and the curtains opened to the unmistakable sound of a Merlin engine as a lone Hurricane zoomed out of the clouds. Within minutes I was totally immersed in a motion picture which has dominated my life for the past 30 years.

While I look on myself as a *Battle of Britain* film 'enthusiast', I am very aware that I am not alone in this 'affliction', and that really is the main reason for writing this book. Many fans of the film were not even born when it was released in 1969, and do not know fully of the immense struggle which took place to get the production up onto the silver screen.

This tome is a tribute to a fine piece of film-making and a movie which, in many aircraft enthusiasts' eyes, is an icon of the cinema screen. It is also worth reflecting upon that had the film not been made, would we, today, be able to gaze upon the world's only airworthy Spitfire IA (AR213) and the sole airworthy Spitfire IIA (P7350) which took part in the real Battle of Britain? For just those two airframes alone, we have to thank *Battle of Britain*.

Robert J. Rudhall, 2000

Reel 2

Opening Shots

The last year of the 1960s was a momentous year. It was the year that man first set foot on the Moon. The Apollo 11 mission with Neil Armstrong, 'Buzz' Aldrin and Michael Collins has gone into the history books and will be engraved in the annals of man's finest achievements forever more. It was also the year that the west's first, and so far, only, supersonic airliner, Concorde, first took to the air. These two 'firsts' captured the imagination of millions of people throughout the world. However, for many aviation enthusiasts, the year 1969 was significant for another reason. It was the year which saw the release of the much-awaited film, *Battle of Britain*.

Many films have been made which have dealt with aerial warfare, several of which have focussed on aspects and areas of the Battle of Britain in 1940, *First of the Few*, *The Way to the Stars*, *Angels One Five* and *Reach For The Sky* being just four British productions which immediately spring to mind. Up until United Artist's *Battle of Britain* no one film had covered the 'Battle' in its entirety. This was the aim of Harry Saltzman and Benjamin S. Fisz, but the struggle to put the 'Battle' onto the silver screen would prove to be a huge one!

The original idea for the film came from Ben S. Fisz, a former RAF fighter pilot, and it was he who kick started the project in the mid-1960s. Fisz had just finished making the film *Heroes of Telemark*, which starred Kirk Douglas, Richard Harris and Michael Redgrave, and was in the process of getting his next production up and running. It was a film about the life of General Orde Wingate, of Chindit fame. The film was almost 'ready to roll', when the Wingate family insisted that they have control over the finished product. If they did not like it then they could legally refuse the film's release. As Fisz remembered at the time: "You cannot spend four million pounds on a possibility, so the whole project fell through."

This was September 1966 and as Fisz walked through Hyde Park in an attempt to console himself after the Wingate setback, his thoughts

A replica Spitfire at Hawkinge. (*PAC*)

turned to the time when a lone Hurricane and Spitfire used to lead the annual Battle of Britain flypast over the City of London each September.

These two vintage fighters were operated by the Royal Air Force's Historic Aircraft Flight, later to become known as the Battle of Britain Flight (now Battle of Britain Memorial Flight). However, due to an engine failure, which caused Spitfire XVI SL574 to force land on Bromley cricket pitch on 20 September 1959, this practice of flying single-engined aircraft over the capital city was brought to a halt.

The idea therefore, as has been published in many previous accounts of the making of *Battle of Britain*, that Fisz was inspired by watching the Hurricane and Spitfire practising for the London flypast, is a figment of 'journalistic licence', and never actually happened.

These memories of the two vintage fighters set Fisz mulling over the idea of a film about the events of 1940, made along the same lines as the very successful movie *The Longest Day*. This 1962 film portrayed both sides of D-Day, June 6, 1944, with the English speaking English and the Germans speaking German, while being subtitled on screen. The idea was a flash of brilliance, but Fisz's task of putting the Battle of Britain

6 Battle of Britain: The Movie

onto film would prove to be fraught with many problems, not least of which was raising the studio backing and finance to realise his dream!

The Telemark film had been distributed by the Rank Organisation, and was reasonably successful, so Fisz contacted Freddie Thomas at Pinewood and put his new proposal to him. Showing interest, Thomas stipulated that Fisz should use the book *The Narrow Margin*, of which Rank owned the screen rights, as the basis for the film's storyline, and that while the Rank Organisation would put up some of the finance required for the production, Fisz would have to raise the rest. The 'blue touch paper' had been lit and Fisz was galvanised into action. He soon gathered together the money needed to set things in motion and *Battle of Britain* was underway.

From the outset, it was decided that the film would be shot in widescreen and in colour, so there would be no opportunity to re-use any wartime newsreel footage in the aerial scenes. This of course meant that a suitable number of vintage aircraft had to be sought in order to make the whole film credible. The problem was, where in the 1960s could enough

'Battle' operated two two-seater Spitfires, this being Tr.9 MJ772 (G-AVAV) in the Henlow line-up. (*Gary Brown Collection* [*GBC*])

airworthy Second World War aircraft be found to recreate the Royal Air Force and Luftwaffe of 1940?

> "For the benefit of the uneducated among us, I'll translate."
> *Edward Fox*

Previous aviation films had used just three or four aircraft, and with the aid of clever camera angles and special effects, tried to give the impression that a large number of aircraft were taking part. This was not good enough for Ben Fisz. He had to have large numbers of real aircraft, otherwise the effect he was looking for just would not work. During the 1960s there was one man the film industry turned to when it needed old aircraft, Group Captain T.G. 'Hamish' Mahaddie.

Hamish was a former RAF Bomber Command pilot, and founder member of the famous Pathfinder Force. He had joined the RAF in 1928, under the Lord Trenchard apprentice scheme. After three years training at RAF Halton he passed out as AC1 – Metal Rigger. Going on to train as a pilot in Egypt, he was eventually posted to 35 Squadron at Abu Sueir. Returning to the UK in 1938, war clouds were looming and on the outbreak of the Second World War he flew a Whitley bomber on the first leaflet-dropping raid of the war. He and his crew were the only ones from the squadron to return from that raid!

Having survived his first tour in Bomber Command, Hamish spent some 20 months training prospective bomber pilots at RAF Kinloss. After this he was selected for the newly formed Pathfinders, in August 1942, joining 7 Squadron as Flight Commander. It was during this period that Hamish had a narrow escape, when Short Stirling R9273, *C for Charlie*, which he was piloting, was attacked by a Junkers Ju 88 night-fighter. Raking the Stirling's fuselage with cannon fire, the enemy aircraft pressed home its devastating attack. With his aileron controls severed by the enemy aircraft's cannon fire, Hamish fought to regain control of the stricken bomber. With judicious use of the engine throttles Mahaddie regained control of the Stirling, bringing it back to the UK, despite another night-fighter attack en route. On inspection of the bomber the following morning, a remarkable 174 cannon shell holes were counted in the Stirling's airframe. From then on, the aircraft was nicknamed *C for Colander*!

8 Battle of Britain: The Movie

The Battle of Britain Flight's Spitfire Mk VB, AB910 was used in the film and seen here being prepared for an airshow appearance in 1968. (*PAC*)

Completing a tour Hamish was then 'hijacked', as he used to put it, to Don Bennett's headquarters, where he was put to work travelling around the various bomber bases selecting crews for the Pathfinder Force. Promoted to the rank of Group Captain, Mahaddie took over command of RAF Warboys, the Pathfinder Force training unit, where he remained until the end of the war. Staying in the RAF Hamish introduced the English Electric Canberra into RAF Bomber Command with his wing at Binbrook. In the mid-1950s he was tasked with 'sourcing' the Avro Lancasters which were to be used in the *The Dambusters* feature film. This was his first foray into the world of films, and he took to it like a duck to water.

He retired from the military in 1959, and almost immediately set up an aviation consultancy for the movie business. By the time *Battle of Britain* came along he had already been involved in a number of productions, *633 Squadron*, *Operation Crossbow*, *The Liquidator*, plus a number of the James Bond films. In a 1988 interview with the author, Hamish recalled his time on *Battle of Britain*: "I was asked by the producers how many

Spitfires were in airworthy condition and could be made available for the film. At that time, I knew of only one, the aircraft that used to fly up the Mall on Battle of Britain Day in September. I was hired and given the task of ascertaining how many real aircraft could be used in the production. Within ten days I had found out that there were over 100 Spitfires still left in the world. They were not all airworthy, but they had possibilities. This was the start of a three-year stint for me. It took 18 months to two years to acquire all of the aircraft, and then a year during which the film was in production."

Mahaddie entered into negotiations with the Ministry of Defence for the loan of a number of Spitfires and Hurricanes, plus some German aircraft, which were preserved with the Air Historical Branch. At that time, it was thought that the RAF would be able to provide all the aircraft needed for the film. While Hamish was scurrying around trying to sort the aircraft out, problems were arising at the Rank Organisation. Costs for the film, which after all was still some way off shooting, were rising rapidly, and rumblings were coming out of the Rank studios that they wanted to have more control over what was being done.

Ben Fisz was obviously not happy about this situation, after all it was his idea in the first place. Other problems were looming on the horizon. Sir Terrance Rattigan, who had been chosen to provide the script, pulled out because of the effect that delays were having on his other work commitments. Lewis Gilbert (*Reach for the Sky*, *Albert RN* and *Sink the Bismarck*) had been earmarked as director, but he too had to move on to other projects due to the frustrating delays in Battle's schedule.

> **"Get that bowser out of here, we'll go on what we've got."**
> *Robert Shaw*

The problems that Fisz was suffering had, in the meantime, come to the attention of Harry Saltzman, master showman (along with Albert R. 'Cubby' Broccoli) of the James Bond film series. Harry contacted Ben Fisz and offered to part finance *Battle*. With the worldwide success of the 007 films, Saltzman had money available, which was a godsend for Fisz, whose problems were starting to be insurmountable. With this newly formed partnership, one of the first things to do was to set up a holding company for the film's production. The aptly named Spitfire Productions

Ltd swiftly came into being, and the film was up on its feet and ready to roll.

One of the first major moves that Saltzman made was to suggest Guy Hamilton as producer of the film. Hamilton had just completed *Funeral in Berlin* for Saltzman and at that time was available. In the realms of film directing Hamilton's pedigree was impeccable. A former assistant to that great British director Sir Carol Reed, with whom he worked on *Fallen Idol* and *The Third Man*, Hamilton also worked with that doyen of producers, John Houston, on the Humphrey Bogart film *The African Queen*.

Guy's first directorial success was *The Colditz Story*, after which he had put his mark on *The Devil's Disciple*, *A Touch of Larceny* and the Bond film *Goldfinger*. Following *Battle of Britain* he went on to direct three more 007 films, *Diamonds Are Forever*, *Live and Let Die* and *The Man With The Golden Gun*, plus *Force Ten From Navarone* and *Evil Under The Sun*.

Having served on Motor Torpedo Boats during the Second World War, Hamilton at first was unsure about directing an aircraft dominated film such as *Battle of Britain*, but, after carrying out extensive research

Avro Lancaster-like engine nacelles, owing to the CASA's Merlin engines, are evident in this shot of one of the two CASA111s which flew to the UK for filming in 1968. (*PAC*)

on the subject, he became totally absorbed. Like the two producers, he wanted to get across both sides of the conflict, telling the story almost in documentary fashion.

"I spent two years of my life on that film", Guy Hamilton recalled in a 1989 interview. "The one thing that I remember distinctly is that wherever we went to get some information or help, the response was fantastic. Everyone had a sort of wartime spirit, and they all wanted to help *Battle of Britain* in one way or another. People came out of retirement and helped us at weekends, their enthusiasm was tremendous. This in turn gave one a great sense of responsibility, in that one felt that the film had to be right. Looking back, I'm proud of the film in the sense that it is honest, or was as honest as we could make it at the time."

In collaboration with writers James Kennaway, and later Wilfred Greatorex, Hamilton set to work on the script, looking at original records, archive film and speaking to a whole host of leading figures on both sides of the 1940 battle. Then disaster struck. On 23 September 1966 the Rank Organisation wrote to Fisz saying that they were pulling out of the production, thus leaving the producers without a distribution company for the film. Negotiations were rapidly entered into with Paramount Pictures in the USA, who expressed an interest in taking the project on. Sadly, differences between Saltzman, Fisz and the powers that be at Paramount saw the studio pull out of any arrangements to finance the film. Nobody seemed to be interested in an all-British war epic in the mid-1960s. Unless a backer could be found the whole project was washed up and going nowhere.

> "Don't threaten or dictate to us until you're marching up Whitehall, and even then we won't listen."
> *Sir Ralph Richardson*

Harry Saltzman knew United Artists (UA) well; after all it was UA which distributed the James Bond films, a series which had made a considerable amount of money for the producers and the distributors alike. After a series of meetings with UA, Harry Saltzman announced that the distribution of *Battle* had been secured, UA would oversee its worldwide release and put a substantial amount of money up front so that production could begin. During this hiatus, when the film lost its major backer when Rank pulled out, virtually all of the staff engaged on *Battle* were made redundant, with the exception of Hamish Mahaddie, who was continuing to scour the world for aircraft.

In a series of meetings, which took place at the highest level within the Ministry of Defence and the Treasury, Mahaddie had, in the meantime, somehow managed to pull off an incredible deal, which saw 19 Spitfires and three Hurricanes being made available to the film company. This arrangement came along with facilities at RAF Henlow, for aircraft conversion purposes, plus the co-operation of the aircraft from the RAF's Battle of Britain Flight, which would take part in the filming schedule between their usual airshow commitments. A number of RAF tradesmen and fitters would also be attached to the film company, for the purposes of maintaining the aircraft while in the company's care. This level of co-operation from the RAF set a precedent, for no film, before or since *Battle of Britain*, has enjoyed such a high input from the military services. It was no doubt due in a large part to Hamish's influence and good standing with the RAF.

The condition of the Spitfires and Hurricanes that Mahaddie had managed to secure, was giving cause for concern. Most of them came from RAF stations throughout the UK, where they had been put to use as gate guards. The majority were late war variants, which would be visually out of character with the early 1940-look that the film makers were trying to convey. This meant that a large amount of work had to take place before the fighters would even be ready for the cameras. At Henlow a 'production line' was set up for converting the aircraft. Hurricanes did not need any cosmetic change work, as the basic outline of the famous Hawker design, more or less, remained unchanged throughout the war. But the Spitfires were another matter entirely.

The Spitfires loaned by the MoD were indeed a mixed bunch of many different marks, and after inspection a compromise was agreed upon, in that all of the non-airworthy aircraft would resemble a cross between a Spitfire V and IX. On the film set this mythical mark was known as the *Mark Addie*, after Hamish's influence in the decision. The engineering team set to work on the Spitfires. The Spitfire XVIs required the most work, cannons had to be removed from the wings, teardrop canopies were taken off, the low-back rear fuselages built up to early high-back configuration by means of an aluminium decking which sat on top of

Vivian Bellamy's 'Proctor – Stuka', known on set as the 'Proctuka' – which was not ultimately used in the film. (*PAC*)

the Spitfire's rear fuselage, pointed rudders were replaced by the standard more rounded design, and clipped wings were restored to their full elliptical status. Where possible four bladed propellers were replaced with three blade units.

Rear view mirrors proved to be a problem, but as Hamish once recalled: "We noticed that the current MG open-top sports car was fitted with a rectangular rear-view mirror, which looked very similar to what we needed for the Spitfires. Mysteriously all of the MGs parked in the carpark at Elstree Film Studios somehow lost their mirrors on one occasion. I'm not quite sure how this happened, but it certainly solved our problem with the Spitfires!"

As work was carried out on the Spitfires, one example, IIA P7350, was found to be in very good condition, so much so that it was deemed possible to put it back into flyable condition for the film. This historic airframe had been on static display at the RAF Colerne Museum for many years, after being saved from the scrap-man. Actually serving with the RAF during the Battle of Britain in 1940, it had flown with 266 and 603 Squadrons, picking up some bullet holes during a dogfight with Messerschmitt Bf 109s in October of that year. This clash with the enemy resulted in a crash landing for P7350, ending its involvement in the Battle of Britain. At the end of the war, it was sold for scrap, but was donated back to the RAF when the scrap merchant realised the historical significance of the airframe.

On display at Colerne for many years, Hamish and his team came across the Spitfire in 1967. With the three-blade propeller, short nose, and early radiator and oil cooler configuration, it was just the sort of Spitfire they had been looking for. Despite previous incorrect accounts of the Spitfire being 'ready to fly after a change of spark plugs and oil', the fighter was given a major overhaul before any attempt was made to fly it again. Although Hurricanes outnumbered Spitfires during the 1940 Battle, they were much harder to find for the film. However, they could not be ignored, as they were needed for the Battle of France sequences at the start of the film, as Spitfires were never sent to France in 1940.

The RAF were only able to provide three Hurricanes, one of which (LF363) was airworthy with the Battle of Britain Flight, LF751 was a gate guardian at Bentley Priory and P2617, which was with the RAF Exhibition Flight. Hurricane PZ865 (G-AMAU) was maintained in airworthy condition by Hawker Siddeley, as part of the company's historic flight, along with Hawker Hart 'J9941' (G-AMBR) and Cygnet G-EBMB, and was made available to the film makers.

A surprise addition to the ranks of Hurricanes came from Canada, in the form of airworthy Mk.XII, CF-SMI. This airframe was originally built by the Canadian Car and Foundry Company at Fort William (now known as Thunder Bay), and served with the Royal Canadian Air Force as RCAF 5377. It was one of a handful of Hurricanes used by British Commonwealth Air Training Plan bases for chasing high altitude Japanese fire balloons. It is also believed that the aircraft served for short periods with 133 and 135 Squadrons, RCAF.

Struck off charge at the end of the war, the Hurricane was discovered many years later in an almost derelict condition by Canadian warbird restorer Robert Diemert, who proceeded to restore it to flying condition. At the completion of the rebuild, Diemart flew the fighter on a regular basis, until it was sold to Hamish Mahaddie on behalf of Spitfire Productions. The Hurricane was flown across the Atlantic inside the hold of a RCAF C-130 Hercules transport aircraft, and re-assembled at Henlow on arrival. Allocated the British civil registration of G-AWLW, the fighter was flown extensively throughout the filming by Diemert himself.

The film's sixth Hurricane (Z7015) came from the Shuttleworth Collection at Old Warden Aerodrome in Bedfordshire. It was hoped to get this rare Sea Hurricane Ib variant into airworthy condition, but persistent problems with an overheating radiator put paid to the film-makers' aims. It was suitable for taxying duties however.

During the long negotiations with the MoD regarding the loan of the Hurricanes and Spitfires, Hamish was also in the process of acquiring civilian-owned flying examples for the extensive aerial sequences. At that stage it became obvious that a team of civilian aircraft engineers would be required to maintain the company's aircraft, as well as lending a hand with the RAF-owned machines. Probably the best company qualified to fulfil the requirement at that time was Simpson's Aero Services, based at Elstree Airfield. Led by John 'Tubby' Simpson, this small organisation

Duxford, 1968: a 'Heinkel', 16 'Me 109s' and three Hurricanes; ten Spitfires were also present but out of shot. (*PAC*)

had an enviable reputation for being able to keep any Merlin-engined aircraft in the air.

> "Undercarriage lever a bit sticky, was it sir?"
> *Duncan Lamont*

While the acquisition of the film's Royal Air Force was proceeding apace, Hamish's thoughts turned to the German Luftwaffe. The small clutch of aircraft loaned by the MoD to the film company (Junkers Ju 88, Junkers Ju 87 Stuka, Heinkel HE 111H and Messerschmitt Bf 109G-2) were in no way airworthy, but would be possibly suitable for static use. To make the film worthwhile Mahaddie had to find a suitable number of German bombers and fighters, otherwise it was doubtful if the effect the producers wanted on screen could be realised.

Thankfully, the Spanish Air Force would come up trumps. Mahaddie was told by one of his contacts that the Spaniards were still using Messerschmitts and Heinkels some 20-odd years after the war had ended. Eager to follow up this important lead Hamish contacted Group Captain R.L.S. Coulson, the Air Attaché at the British Embassy in Madrid, immediately who, after some enquiries, confirmed the existence

A unique sight: nine 'Me 109' *Buchons* at Manston guarded by an MoD police officer. (*PAC*)

of the German aircraft. Hamish flew out to Spain straight away to see for himself, hardly believing his own eyes when he found the Spanish Air Force's main bomber force was still comprised of Merlin-engined Heinkels. Unfortunately, the Messerschmitts he had expected to see alongside the bombers had been retired about one year earlier. However, after asking a few questions in the right places Hamish found a great pile of dismantled Messerschmitts lying behind a couple of hangars at Tablada Airfield.

How these Heinkels and Messerschmitts happened to be in Spain in the first-place needs some explaining.

During the Spanish Civil War, Germany supplied 96 Heinkel 111s, and those left at the end of the conflict were transferred to the Ejercito del Aire (Spanish Air Force). During the Second World War the Spanish authorities started negotiations with Germany to purchase another 50 examples, plus a licence to build the twin-engined bomber in Spain. The Germans agreed to this and a further 70 Heinkels duly arrived in Spain from Germany. Subsequently a licence was drawn up for the local production of 130 airframes to be constructed by Construccions Aeronauticas SA (CASA) at Tablada, near Seville, with the designation CASA 2.111. Emerging in three basic variants, bomber, reconnaissance and transport, the Heinkels served up to the end of the Second World War, by which time the Spaniards had put plans into motion to re-engine the aircraft, due to earlier difficulties in obtaining from Germany suitable supplies of Junkers Jumo engines; 173 Rolls-Royce Merlin 500 engines were acquired from the UK, with the intention of re-engining the best 70 aircraft of the remaining fleet. This programme was carried out on the Heinkels between 1953 and 1956. With no other suitable type available, the Spanish Heinkels soldiered on through to the 1960s, and some 32 were still in service by the time that Hamish caught up with them in mid-1966.

It was a similar story for the Messerschmitt 109s. Germany had delivered 25 dismantled airframes, minus engines, propellers, tailplanes and armament, to Spain during the Second World War, originally intending to complete the consignment. Time went on and the war took a turn for the worse for Germany, so much so that the missing Messerschmitt parts never arrived. These airframes were intended to act as pattern aircraft for future Spanish production. The Spaniards then found themselves with a set of incomplete aircraft, and no manufacturing jigs or drawings.

By the end of 1944 it was obvious that the missing parts were never going to arrive, so the Spanish authorities took matters into their own hands and installed a recently tested Hispano-Suiza 12Z 89 engine into one of the Messerschmitt Bf 109E-1 airframes. The end result of the German airframe and the Spanish engine did not prove to be entirely suitable, but at that time there were no other options available. This prototype conversion, designated as Hispano HA-1109 J1L flew for the first time in this guise on March 2, 1945. Conversion of the Bf 109G airframes then commenced, with some 25 being carried out over the following 18 months.

This combination proved to be less than satisfactory, so much so that the converted aircraft were not even issued to the Spanish Air Force. Subsequent modifications saw the French-built Hispano Suiza 12Z 12 fuel injected engine being installed in the 10th Hispano HA 1109 J1L, being designated as the prototype HA 1109 K1L. This proved to be a much more satisfactory arrangement and production deliveries started in earnest during 1952. During 1953 it was decided to adapt the Messerschmitt airframe to take the tried and tested Rolls-Royce Merlin engine, and this proved to be the ultimate variant of Willy Messerschmitt's famous fighter. It was ironic to say the least that the famed Bf 109 first flew under the power of a Rolls-Royce engine (Kestrel) and its last variant would be fitted with the breed of engine which was fitted to its deadly wartime enemy, the Spitfire! 1954 saw the first Merlin-engined Messerschmitt 109 take to the air, a feat that it accomplished from San Pablo Airport, near Seville.

It was the Hispano HA 1112 M1L Buchon variant of the famed fighter that Hamish Mahaddie gazed upon behind the hangars at Tablada in 1966. The type had remained in service with the Spaniards, providing effective ground attack and fighter capabilities right up to the mid-1960s. After inspection it was ascertained that 27 complete aircraft could be made from all the bits that lay around on the airfield, of which 18 would be able to fly, with the remainder capable of taxying or being used as static dressing for airfield scenes.

The 'Messerschmitts' were about to come up for sale in an auction, or as it is known in Spain, a Sabasta. Hamish would remember that word long after the film was a fading memory, for it was a make or break crisis during his involvement with *Battle*. A Sabasta is a sealed bid auction,

Spitfire PR.XIX PS853 was one of three airworthy Griffon-engined Spitfires used in the film. (*PAC*)

and after consultation with the authorities, as to the price range they were expecting to realise on the aircraft (around $2,250 each), Hamish entered his bid only to be confronted by a rival consortium who were also interested in the Messerschmitts, and who were obviously trying to push the price up. Following many telephone calls to various contacts in high places Mahaddie did not alter his bid, and on the day of the auction came away with the Messerschmitts as one job lot.

As for the Heinkels, they were still in service and were obviously not for sale. Would it therefore be possible for the film company to 'borrow' the bombers in order to shoot the Luftwaffe sequences in the movie? Sadly for the film makers, this was a period when Anglo-Spanish relations were at a low ebb. Wrangling over the ownership of Gibraltar had reached a peak, and here was a film company asking to borrow the entire Spanish bomber fleet.

It took some high-level diplomacy by British officials, Saltzman, Fisz and Mahaddie to save the day on that score. Initially General Franco refused permission for the Heinkels to be used, but after considerable pressure from Rolls-Royce, who, after all, supplied the much-needed spares for the engines, Franco relented and gave his permission. Eventually, after much to-ing and fro-ing of official documents between the British and Spanish governments, it was agreed that Spitfire Productions could use the Heinkels, and that all costs involved regarding fuel and maintenance, crews' wages etc, would be covered by the Spanish government. The only exception being that the film company would have to pay for the painting of the aircraft in German markings, and then return them to Spanish colours when the filming was finished.

This was a major breakthrough for Saltzman and Fisz, and the unprecedented level of co-operation from Spain is reported to have saved the film around £200,000. After many hurdles, *Battle of Britain* had gained its Luftwaffe! Back in the UK, Spitfires were still being rounded up to star in the film. Air Commodore Allen Wheeler's Mk Ia AR213 (G-AIST), which had been in storage at Old Warden Aerodrome for several years, was re-assembled and made ready by 'Tubby' Simpson and his crew. The Shuttleworth Collection's Spitfire V, AR501 (G-AWII), was rejuvenated and added to the 'squadron'. Spitfire IX MH434

Hurricane IIC LF363 wearing Polish colours for the film. (*PAC*)

(G-ASJV) had been purchased from Tim Davies, a pair of former Irish Air Corps two-seat Spitfire trainers, MJ772 (G-AVAV) and TE308 (G-AWGB), owned by Tony Samuelson at Elstree, had also been put under contract, and would prove to be especially useful in the training up of the pilots who were to fly the vintage fighters in the film, as well as acting as camera platforms for specific scenes.

Rolls-Royce's Griffon-engine Mk XIV RM689 (G-ALGT) was leased to the film company, and a similar deal was reached with the Texas-based Confederate Air Force (CAP), which had just purchased Spitfire IX MK297 (G-ASSD) in the UK and four of the Messerschmitts in Spain. A proviso in the contract stated that this quintet would be flown in the film by CAP pilots, Wilson 'Connie' Edwards, Marvin 'Lefty' Gardner, Milt Harradence, Gerald Martin and Lloyd Nolen. A further Spitfire IX, MH415 (G-AVDJ) came out of storage in France. All of these had to be prepared for filming by Simpson's Aero Services at RAF Henlow, and painted in 1940 camouflage.

While a lot of emphasis was being put on the aircraft to be used in the production, the two producers had also been busy signing up actors and actresses for the 'human' side of the story. Sir Lawrence Olivier was contracted to play the vital part of Air Chief Marshal Hugh Dowding, Rex Harrison was originally cast for the part of Air Vice-Marshal Keith Park, but had to drop out due to delays in production. His place was taken by Trevor Howard. Squadron Commanders came in the shape of Michael Caine, Christopher Plummer and Robert Shaw, while some of Britain's up and coming actors would play the younger pilots, James Cosmo, Edward Fox, David Griffin, Myles Hoyle and Ian McShane. Personifying key diplomatic representatives were Sir Ralph Richardson and Curt Jurgens, while smaller, but no less important, roles were taken by Kenneth More, Nigel Patrick, Michael Redgrave and Patrick Wymark. The sole major female part, and the film's obligatory love interest, was given to Susannah York. The 'acting' content of the film was indeed in the 'heavyweight' class.

> "Spring chicken to shite hawk in one easy lesson."
> *Edward Fox*

Work was carrying on in Spain to put the non-airworthy Messerschmitt fighters back into flying condition. The Spanish Air Force mechanics worked hard to ensure that the required number of 109s were ready for the filming to begin. $1,000 was allocated to each of the airworthy examples, and $600 for the taxying machines. The Spanish-built Messerschmitt was a radically different beast from the German Bf 109E variant, which fought in the 1940 Battle. Now fitted with the Merlin, the entire nose contour had been changed. There was little the film company could do about this, but it could re-model other areas of the Messerschmitts to be as close to the E model as possible.

The paint scheme would be a great help in disguising the Buchon, but there were other 'specifics' which could be tackled as well. Dummy machine guns were fitted to the wings, the upper engine cowling had a couple of replica machine guns mounted, and 109E-style tail struts were added to the rear fuselage. But there was one important area which would make all the difference on screen.

Hamish Mahaddie takes up the story: "In order to give a clear definition between the RAF and the Luftwaffe, we had the beautiful elliptical shape of the Spitfire's wing, and the cut off squared-look of the Messerschmitt. But the 109 built by the Spanish had nearly a metre of rounded wingtip. In charge of flying the Messerschmitts for the filming was Comandante Pedro Santa Cruz, and he was not all happy when I suggested removing the round wingtips.

"I said that I would personally test the de-tipped Messerschmitt, and this was tantamount to an insult to a Spaniard, especially one of his ability, to say you will do something after inferring he cannot do it. Santa Cruz became very annoyed with me and said 'Certainly not, El Hamish', as he called me, 'I will do the testing'. We then removed the wingtips, faired the ends over and true to his word, Santa Cruz test flew the fighter, and was actually ecstatic about the performance of the aircraft, asking why the rounded wingtips had been fitted in the first place!"

By late 1967 arrangements had been made with the Spaniards to use the airfield at Tablada to represent Germany and France in the film. The production was ready to roll and a first shooting date of Spring 1968 had been set by the producers and director. *Battle of Britain* was, at long last, underway.

Reel 3

Film Logistics

To make a film on the scale of *Battle of Britain* was a massive undertaking. Both producers were well aware of the immense expense of launching into a project such as this, but to the ordinary film fan in the street, to comprehend the many 'behind the scenes' arrangements which have to be met if the production is to function, is difficult to say the least.

This can probably be served best by reproducing a Spitfire Productions memo (Company's proposals for mounting the flying effort) which was circulated on 1 February 1968, with regard to the Ministry of Defence support requested for the movie. This gives some idea of the scale of the operations needed to put the 1940 conflict onto the cinema screen:

Spitfire Mk IIA P7350 was an actual Battle of Britain veteran, during which it was damaged in combat, and also flew for the film. (*PAC*)

Aerial Filming
This is planned to take place over the three months, May to July 1968, the intensive phase being during June and July. All filming at RAF airfields will take place during daylight hours and from Monday to Friday only.

Aircraft
9 Spitfires, 3 Hurricanes and 18 Me 109s, 3 He 111s, 3 Stuka/Proctor conversions, 1 helicopter and 1 B-25 photographic aircraft will be used. None of these aircraft belong to the Spanish Air Force: most are company-owned and the remainder are on loan from various non-Spanish sources. These aircraft will operate under civil licence and Board of Trade Certificates of Airworthiness are being obtained. In addition, the Company hope that the flying effort provided by these aircraft will be supplemented from time to time during the three months, May to July, by the RAF Memorial Flight (3 Spitfires and 1 Hurricane).

Operational Base
All the civil aircraft would for the most part operate from RAF Duxford – an inactive station – and be serviced there. The RAF Memorial Flight would normally operate from its home base (Coltishall).

Aircraft Servicing
This will be the responsibility of Simpson's Aero Services, under contract let by the film company, the aircraft will be serviced to Board of Trade regulations which are said to be even more stringent than those applicable in the Royal Air Force. Although the servicing company have sufficient licensed civil engineers (management staff), they do not possess the necessary skilled manpower at the supervisory levels and would have the greatest difficulty in recruiting this skilled manpower for such a short-term task.

Therefore, the film company propose that RAF tradesmen should fill the gap. These tradesmen would be required mainly for the supervision of Simpsons' junior fitters and mechanics (mainly ex-Servicemen) on the daily maintenance of the Spitfires, Hurricanes and Me 109s, but would work as 'producers' when necessary. Work on the Me 109 aircraft would be supervised mainly by Spanish Air Force engineers who would be on unpaid leave and in civilian uniforms.

Control of Flying Operations
Flying is planned to commence on a limited scale from Duxford on the 1st May 1968, with the intensive phase taking place from the 1st June to the 31st July. The film company propose that an RAF Wing Commander should be in control of the intensive flying operations and would be directly responsible to the film director for the execution of all flying sequences. His pilots would comprise British test pilots, ex-American and ex-Canadian Air Force and Spanish Air Force pilots in civilian guise, supplemented by a number of RAF pilots (QFI's in Flying Training Command). By having an RAF Wing Commander in charge, this should ensure that operations are conducted strictly in accordance with RAF procedures.

Conversion to Type
Conversion to type will be carried out as follows: the company have a dual control Me 109 and Spitfire. One RAF QFI will be converted to the Me 109 by the Chief Pilot of the Spanish company who serviced the Me 109s for the Spanish Air Force. One RAF QFI will be converted to the Spitfire by a QFI of the Memorial flight. These two QFI will then convert the rest of the RAF pilots to the Me 109 and Spitfire. The RAF pilots who will fly the Hurricanes will be given a briefing by the RAF Memorial flight Hurricane pilot. All the other aircraft involved will be flown by civil pilots, and these pilots, American, Canadian, Spanish and British, are very experienced on the types concerned.

Air Traffic Control
Arrangements are in hand with the National Air Traffic Control services for provision of air space for the aerial filming and it has been agreed that the Military Air Traffic Organisation should exercise air traffic control of all flying undertaken in connection with the film. Flying will be conducted strictly in accordance with current military regulations. Thus, there will be no unauthorised low flying or any other infringements of aviation rules likely to cause annoyance to other aviators or to the public.

Hurricanes! (*PAC*)

Control of RAF Personnel
The RAF Project Officer will command the personnel on loan to the company and would be responsible for their discipline and welfare. They will be accommodated at a nearby RAF station (probably Bassingbourn) who will provide full parenting facilities.

Accommodation at Henlow
Three small hangars and office accommodation for the refurbishing of vintage aircraft – flying and non-flying – for use in the production of the film. This accommodation will be required until about the 1st May 1968.

Airfields
The inactive RAF airfield at Duxford including several buildings for the period 1st February to 31st August (7 months) as the main base from which aerial activity will take place. Filming activities are also required at other airfields which are currently being assessed for suitability by the film director. These will probably be Bicester, Debden, Cardington and North Weald – the latter was transferred to the Army Department. With the exception of North Weald, filming activity will be on a small scale mainly to provide different backgrounds. Therefore, interference with normal RAF operations is unlikely.

Vehicles – Required at Duxford
1st May to 15th August. (For Airfield Safety Service) 1 Mk 5 or Mk 6 Fire truck, 1 dual purpose Fire/Crash truck, 1 Landrover, 1 Ambulance. (For conveyance of stores and personnel) 1 passenger/cargo van, 1 minicar. (For towing aircraft and ground purposes) 2 Light tractors.

Parachutists
6 volunteer parachutists are required between 10th and 17th June and 8th and 15th July for scenes showing German and British aircrews abandoning their aircraft over English countryside and the sea. The precise method of shooting these scenes has yet to be settled, but we have suggested that the parachutists should be filmed climbing out of the 109s and Spitfires in a wind tunnel and that the actual jumps should be done from a helicopter above a regular parachute-dropping zone. Control of jumping operations should be vested in the senior RAF parachutist taking part.

These requirements passed through many offices within the RAF and MoD before an agreement was reached. Even then, it was plain that this level of co-operation was not going to come free of charge. There would also be a number of conditions which would have to be met if the film company were to benefit from the full backing of the RAF. A Ministry of Defence document dated 7 March 1968, sent to Spitfire Productions Ltd, set out those terms and conditions needed:

- The initial loan of RAF personnel, operative from 19th February, 1968, consists of 8 engineering tradesmen, supplemented by a further 13 on 11th March, who will carry out their duties at RAF Henlow and later at RAF Duxford (subject to the conclusion of a separate agreement covering the leasing of that station) whilst on loan to your company. Any further RAF personnel (including any extra personnel who may be attached to RAF Bassingbourn in support of loaned personnel, e.g. catering staff) and any supply of vehicles, equipment or aircraft, will be listed as additional annexes to the agreement and will be loaned subject to the same terms and conditions or to such amendments as may be mutually agreed.

28 Battle of Britain: The Movie

- It is estimated that the total costs of supplying the RAF assistance, as itemised, which your company has requested, will be in the region of £139,000. This figure is quoted solely for your guidance and is based on a current assessment of probable costs. It excludes the costs of any additional RAF personnel or other RAF assistance including issues of equipment etc, that may be required from time to time.

This document also laid out the insurance required from Spitfire Productions with regard to the MoD participating aircraft and equipment.

- To effect with an insurance company or companies a policy or policies of insurance covering loss of or damage to historic aircraft provided by the Royal Air Force: each aircraft in a non-flying condition to be insured in the sum of £5,000, and each aircraft from the Royal Air Force Memorial Flight to be insured in the sum of £10,000.

Strict guidelines were also issued regarding the use of RAF personnel and aircraft to be employed during the period of filming.

- The company will accept responsibility for the serviceability of all aircraft serviced by RAF personnel on loan to the company. RAF

Spitfire 'EQ-A' was actually Mk XVI TB382, and 'EQ-F' Mk XVI TE384. (*PAC*)

personnel on loan will not be permitted to certify aircraft as serviceable for flight.
- The company will obtain British certificates of Airworthiness or Permits to Fly for all aircraft (other than those aircraft loaned from the RAF Memorial Flight) used for flying during the production of the film in accordance with Board of Trade rules.
- RAF aircraft on loan to the company (other than those of the RAF Memorial Flight) will not be flown without the written permission of the Ministry of Defence; RAF aircraft will not be cannibalised for any purpose whatsoever; and RAF pilots only will fly RAF-owned aircraft.

In a separate letter, dated 7 March 1968, the MoD outlined to the film company the use that could be made of the facilities at Duxford. This included:

- Use of Buildings on the Domestic Site – Officers' Mess (38 bedrooms, dining room, billiard room and large ladies' room), Sergeant Pilot Mess (16 rooms), H Block Airmen's Quarters (No's 212, 213, 214) Airmen's Blocks (7, 9, 13), Sergeants' Mess (16 single quarters and annex consisting of 22 single quarters), Airmen's Mess.
- Use of Buildings on the Airfield – Armoury, Air Traffic Control, Carpenters Shop, Old Equipment Section, Station Headquarters, Guard Room, Frontal Offices by Hangars, 4 Hangars, plus use of runways and peri track and bays along the boundary of the airfield.
- The rental assessment, taking into consideration the extensive repair and decorating work which your company will need to carry out at their own expense before the accommodation is suitable for occupation, is as follows: Airfield, hangars and ancillary buildings – £4,000 per month. Domestic Site buildings – £2,000 per month.

While these outlined costings pale into insignificance when it comes to the sums of money expended by film-makers today, it has to be remembered that this was 1967 and the sums of money mentioned above had to be spent before any of the actual filming could begin.

Saltzman and Fisz soon learnt that to produce *Battle of Britain* on the scale demanded to ensure an authentic end product was going to cost them a lot more than they had originally envisaged!

Reel 4

Lights, Cameras, Action!

In January 1968 an advance film construction crew was sent out to Spain to prepare the locations needed for the filming. One of the first areas to be tackled was Huelva beach, near Seville, which would double for Dunkirk in the French evacuation scenes. It was ironic that the film producers should pick Huelva, as it was here that the body of the real 'man who never was' was washed up in 1943. This was a wartime deception tactic by the Allies to fool the Axis forces with false 'top secret' documents about D-Day. The story was later dramatised in the 1955 film *The Man Who Never Was*, with Clifton Webb and Robert Flemyng. The latter would play Wing Commander Willoughby, one of the operations room controllers at AVM Keith Park's (Trevor Howard) headquarters in *Battle of Britain*.

Alterations had to be made at Tablada and El Corpero airfields (*see* On Location), the two main aircraft locations in Spain, and by early March an 85-strong team of accountants, boom operators, camera operators, carpenters, clapper boys, electricians, hairdressers, make-up personnel, painters, riggers, sound mixers, continuity girls and secretaries had been flown out to Spain to start work preparing the main locations for shooting. March 13th saw the first major sequence in the production committed to film. This was the opening title scene, when Dietrich Frauboes, playing the part of Feldmarschall Erhard Milch, inspects the rows of Heinkel bombers.

Before the rehearsals began for the scene there was a two-minute silence observed for Don Federico Eglesias Lanzos, who had been killed on 20 January while flying aerobatics in one of the Messerschmitt 109s. As a mark of respect, the film company paid £18,000 to his widow.

Several rehearsals were needed to get the timings and positions just right for this long sequence in the film, and it was not until mid-afternoon that Guy Hamilton was satisfied with the action and the light conditions for filming. Perched atop the director's podium, Hamilton called 'Action'

Lights, Cameras, Action!

The two airworthy CASA 'He 111s', G-AWHA and G-AWHB, at Duxford during filming in 1968. (*PAC*)

at 3pm and the film was actually underway. This was the first of over 5,000 separate shots, which would eventually go to make up the finished film. After many trials and tribulations, it looked as if the film was finally getting moving and something useful was, at last, going 'into the can'.

> "It's been tried and tested, so don't blame the system if you're no good."
> *Nigel Patrick*

While much attention had been paid to getting the requisite numbers of aircraft on the British and German sides of the story, little thought had seemingly been paid to arranging these aircraft in the air for the cameras. With this in mind the film company was very fortunate to secure the services of one John Blake. John, in subsequent years would be known the world over for his airshow commentaries in the UK and abroad, but at that time he was working for the Royal Aero Club. In a 1999 interview with the author, John fondly remembered how he became involved with *Battle of Britain*:

"The film was on for a while and then off, when the money problems came along, but when they got it cracking again, they came to some minor crisis point at Pinewood, because they needed somebody to come in for a couple of weeks to help out on the film's storyboards. [Storyboards are the drawings of the action as the producers envisage it on screen. These are then studied by the film cameraman to see if what is depicted can actually be achieved before any shooting begins.]

"They wanted someone who knew something about air to air photography, somebody who knew something about flying and someone who knew something about drawing for the storyboards. I had gained experience in all of these fields over the years. Quentin Laurence, who I had known for several years, and who was involved with the film as its Aerial Unit Director, asked me if I wanted to spend a couple of weeks helping them out on the film. I therefore joined the art department at Pinewood, working on the storyboards.

"After a couple of days, I was asked if I could design the fighter and bomber formations for the film. I then produced scale blueprints of the

Heinkel take-off – G-AWHB. (*PAC*)

formations so that the producers could get some idea of what they were going to see on screen. After this another problem reared its head, which was one that the film makers never really solved, and that was how to present a credible looking dogfight on film. I designed a 3D model of a dogfight, which was basically a series of narrow strips of card, following the path of each aircraft, divided into coloured time segments so that you could see where each aircraft would be at a given time. This was received, with some awe and consternation, by the film people, and taken away to be studied. I never ever saw it again.

"In the end the producers took a look at the old Howard Hughes film, *Hell's Angels*, which is notable for its dogfight scenes. It was arranged for Ben Fisz, Guy Hamilton, plus one or two other people fairly high up in the film's production, to watch this film in order to get some ideas on how to come up with the dogfight scenes for *Battle of Britain*. Everybody else involved in the film was warned firmly that this was a private showing and they would not be admitted. There was even a notice on the door of the viewing cinema that this was out of bounds to 'all ranks'.

"However, when the lights went up after the screening, it transpired that the cinema was packed with people who should not have been there in the first place. We had all crept in while the lights were out to watch *Hell's Angels*. Nothing was actually said about this transgression, but it was discovered that all Howard Hughes did on *Hell's Angels* was to line the aircraft up at different distances from the camera and get them to loop and roll, which looked like a dogfight in the finished film.

"I spent about six weeks at Pinewood, working on all manner of things to do with the film. I was called in to one of the meetings involving those people who were going to go out to Spain for the mass bomber sequences. Sitting opposite me was an old friend, John 'Jeff' Hawke, who was flying the camera aircraft for the filming, and, largely at his and Quentin's suggestion, I ended up being asked to go to Spain with the flying unit in order to give the daily briefings. This took up a further two months, so what started out as a quick two-week job actually took a considerable time."

> "More accurate the other way round,
> I'm trusting in God and praying for Radar."
> *Sir Laurence Olivier*

In order to capture on film scenes of the RAF attacking large formations of Luftwaffe aircraft, the producers decided that one of the company's Spitfires would have to fly out to Spain in order to participate in these scenes. Spitfire IX MH415 (G-AVDJ) was the aircraft chosen, and it was duly fitted with a long-range fuel tank so that it had extra 'legs' for the flight. Spitfire Productions contracted the well-known aircraft restorer and replica builder Vivian Bellamy to fly the Spitfire out to Spain, as Vivian's experience on large piston engined fighters was considerable. Bellamy served as a pilot with the Fleet Air Arm during the Second World War, and postwar had owned Spitfire (Tr.8 G-AIDN) for a number of years, before selling it on to his brother-in-law, John Fairey.

At his home in 1997, just a matter of months before he died, Vivian Bellamy recalled his time on the *Battle of Britain* film during an interview with the author:

"Because I had flown this sort of aircraft before, the film company asked me if I could fly the Spitfire out to Spain, and I said yes, no trouble at all. I remember I had a few snags with the drop tank, in that it at first was not 'petrol tight' in the connections between the tank and the aircraft's main fuel system, but we eventually sorted it out. I took off from Eastleigh Airport and flew down, aiming for Biarritz, but it started to rain and the weather slowly got worse. At one time a French Air Force Mystère jet came alongside me to take a look at the old Spitfire. I was doing about 150 knots, and the Mystère had a bit of a job to go as slow as me. He came past with the flaps and undercarriage down at one point. The weather got so bad that I had to turn back and land at Bordeaux. As soon as I taxied in, ancient Frenchmen, who had flown Spitfires at one time or another, surrounded the aircraft.

"The following day I took off bound for Madrid. In years gone by you could almost see Madrid when you climbed to height, but with all the pollution of the 1960s it was a bit of a job sometimes to actually see where you were going. However, I landed safely at Madrid, after which the aircraft was surrounded again, but this time by Germans, who had all turned out to see the famous, or in their eyes, infamous, Spitfire. I decided to show them what a Spitfire could do, so when I took off, I gave the aircraft 18lbs of boost, and it literally shot into the sky, followed by a low flypast down the runway. As I was about to turn on course for

Seville, the airfield control tower came on the radio and said, 'Would you do that again please'.

"When I arrived at Tablada the film company was very pleased to see the aircraft, as by then they were getting a little fed up with the Spaniards and the Messerschmitts, so the sight of a Spitfire really boosted their morale. It was at Tablada that I met Pedro Santa Cruz for the first time and I have to say was very impressed with his skill as a pilot. We let Santa Cruz fly the Spitfire once, and he was very good with it. After he had landed, I asked him what he thought of the famous Spitfire, and he said 'It is a very good aeroplane, but I prefer the Messerschmitt.' But then he would, wouldn't he?

"On one occasion, which I will never forget, we saw Santa Cruz climb into one of the Heinkel bombers and taxi out from the line-up. He then took off and proceeded to carry out some low flypasts over the airfield. He then climbed to height, feathered both propellers and brought the aircraft down very low, actually flying through the gap he had left in the Heinkel line-up, then pull up and re-start the engines before landing back. I could not actually believe my eyes."

One of the two CASA111s cruises down the Thames Estuary ready for the dusk attack on London scene. (*PAC*)

While filming on the ground was relatively easy, it was a different story when the aircraft got airborne. Firstly shooting had to be carried out in reasonably sunny skies, which could be matched with filming back in the UK, secondly all the mass bomber formations had to be carried out over sea, as the landscape of Spain was most unlike that of Kent in 1940, and thirdly time was of the essence, as the Messerschmitts still had the lack of range problem that the Luftwaffe suffered back in 1940.

As John Blake remembered: "We used to fly a racetrack pattern with the Heinkels, and the Messerschmitts were in the standard wartime finger four formation, but considerably closed up so that they would fit into the camera frame. We also used to get the filming sequences all lined up ready, and then a fleet of Spanish fishing trawlers would come into shot below us and we would have to go around again. The aircraft were formed up into two separate blocks of fighters and bombers, codenamed Sevillia and Betis, which were the names of the two local football teams. The bombers would take off and join up over Tablada and head west over the coast, and then fly a long big racetrack pattern, with about a 15-minute duration each side. The 109s came up separately, and joined in where they were required. Quentin Laurence and I spent hours on the floor of one of the hangars at Tablada with a lot of plastic Airfix models on sticks, placing them into the formations required for the filming."

> "This is only the beginning, they won't stop now."
> *Trevor Howard*

Held up for some considerable time due to poor weather conditions, indeed so much rain fell in Spain that Tablada began to resemble a Chinese paddy field on more than one occasion, the filming schedule fell badly behind, and the costs of the production rocketed upwards. The Spanish sequences had to be put 'in the can' quickly before severe money problems started to affect the whole production. Eventually the required flying took place, and the sole Spitfire was gainfully employed diving through the formations of Heinkels numerous times, getting the footage required to match in with the proposed shooting in the UK. Even then things did not always go according to the briefings, as once airborne, radio problems and misunderstandings due to the different languages, often saw a lot of flying time wasted before any useful footage could be obtained.

Mid-way through the Spanish filming the Spanish Air Ministry informed the film company that the entire Heinkel fleet would be needed for a ceremonial flypast during a NATO exercise, which was due to take place in the Atlantic. This would entail removing the German camouflage and markings and replacing them with the Heinkel's original Spanish Air Force colours. With an estimated cost of £1,000 per aircraft, this was the last thing that Spitfire Productions needed at that stage of the production.

The time lost in filming and the extra cost involved could prove to be crippling for Spitfire Productions. Director Guy Hamilton protested in no uncertain terms to the Spanish 'powers that be' and after some heated negotiations it was decided to leave the Heinkels in Luftwaffe markings. Needless to say, it must have been a very unusual sight for the NATO generals to see a mass formation of Second World War Luftwaffe-painted bombers approaching the saluting area!

When the weather was 'playing ball' in Spain, it was a good day if the film company got two air-to-air filming sorties in one day. Normally, by the time the daily briefings had taken place and the weather had been checked it was only possible to carry out one afternoon flight.

One of the most difficult scenes to film was the sequence when Goering and the Luftwaffe 'top brass' were positioned on the edge of the cliffs to watch the mass formations of bombers and fighters flying across the supposedly English Channel to pulverise London. This was supposed to represent the Pas de Calais in Northern France, but was actually filmed about ten miles from Tablada on the edge of a large olive grove. A replica obelisk, representing the one at Cap Blanc Nez, was built on the cliff, but was only clad from the top to a point halfway down the monument, in order to save money. This meant that the camera could only shoot from the halfway point, otherwise the bare scaffolding would show in the finished film. This in turn restricted the area in which the aircraft had to fly for the cameras, and trying to get the mass of aircraft in the correct position for the camera angle proved to be particularly troublesome.

"We set up a special racetrack pattern for this scene", remembers John Blake, "over endless and featureless olive groves, and it was very difficult to actually see this obelisk until you were on top of it. It required some very accurate flying by the Spanish pilots as it had to be carried out at reasonably low level. Through the company's interpreter I asked

Bombs fall on Duxford! (*PAC*)

the formation leader, Colonel Lopez Gomez, who commanded the 7th Bomber Wing of the Spanish Air Force, if he could keep an absolutely accurate course over the obelisk. After a burst of Spanish between the interpreter and the pilot, the interpreter said 'The pilot knows the area very well, he owns all of these olives!'"

The scenes showing Heinkels dropping bombs had to be carried out on one day, due to the fact that all of the film's 'concrete' bombs had to be dropped in 'one lot'. Constructed in Spain by a local company, they cost the film company a lot of money, so much so that it was not possible to have any spares made. It was decided therefore that this could only be a 'one take' option, and there would be no chance for a second bite of the cherry.

As the weather continued to disrupt filming, it was mooted that another option would be to ship the bombs to the UK and drop them over the Wash area if a 'shoot' in Spain was not going to be possible. This idea was thwarted when it was discovered that the Spanish customs authorities would not grant an export licence for the concrete bombs and they had to stay in the country of origin.

"On the allotted bomb-dropping day we flew south", recalled John Blake, "instead of flying our usual westerly direction. The Heinkels set off and actually headed in the direction of Gibraltar. At that time General Franco was having one of his tantrums about the British and Gibraltar, and I did actually wonder whether the Spanish pilots were going to drop the concrete bombs on Gibraltar! Thankfully they didn't and the scenes were shot successfully."

After many frustrating hold ups, the Spanish filming sequences came to an end and the film company packed up its belongings and made ready to return to the UK. Spitfire Productions had, in the meantime, purchased two of the Heinkels from the Spanish Air Force, in order to match in film sequences in England with RAF fighters attacking the Luftwaffe.

By now it was early May, the Spanish filming having taken a lot longer than had been planned. Things had to move fast if the shooting schedule was to be kept on track. The long flight for the Spitfire, the 17 Messerschmitts, two Heinkels and the B-25 Mitchell was planned and scheduled. It would take at least three days to get the aircraft to Duxford, the film company's main base in the UK. By the time the aircraft arrived in England and were made ready for the cameras it would be mid-May and time was indeed pressing. One chapter of the filming had come to an end, another chapter, with even more frustrations to come, was about to begin.

Reel 5

Battle's Camera Ship

To film the all-colour aerial sequences for the movie it was obvious that a special flying camera platform would be required. It had to be one which would be fast enough to be able to keep up with the fighters, and yet be large enough to ably accommodate the Panavision cameras of the film unit.

The producers turned to John 'Jeff' Hawke, who had previously been associated with a number of aviation films. Hawke was a former Royal Air Force Flight Lieutenant, who at one stage was involved in the abortive restoration to flying condition of Messerschmitt Bf 109G-2 *Black Six* at RAF Wattisham in the 1960s, he was also one of the Mosquito pilots during the filming of *633 Squadron*.

During the mid to late 1960s Jeff Hawke was President of an American-based company called Euramericair, which just happened to have recently acquired from Panama, at a reported cost of $11,500, a North American B-25 Mitchell twin-engined bomber, 44-31508 (N6578D). Built as a B-25J-30-NJ, the aircraft was delivered to the United States Army Air Force in June 1945. Post-war it was modified by the Hughes Corporation to TB-25K status. Demobbed from the military it passed through several civilian owners until taken on strength by Euramericair. For the purpose of the *Battle of Britain*'s air to air filming work the Mitchell was much modified. In November 1967 the B-25 flew out of Florida bound for the UK. The Atlantic crossing took a total of 22 hours to complete, and after its arrival in Britain work started on the many modifications to turn the former bomber into a flying film studio.

The two waist gun positions were removed and camera mounts were bolted into place. The bomber's tail gun position was taken out and replaced with an open tail and wind deflector arrangement, which enabled a Panavision camera to be mounted out in the open, aft of the aircraft's fins and rudders. The mid-upper gun turret was taken out and replaced with a large Perspex blister, under which the film's aerial director would

Inevitably, amongst the film's technical advisors was the legendary, legless, Battle of Britain ace, Group Captain Douglas Bader, made a global household name the previous decade through the book and film *Reach for the Sky*. The Group Captain is seen here with admiring young fans on set at Duxford in 1968. (*Historic Military Press* [*HMP*])

sit during shooting of the aerial combat sequences, as Hamish Mahaddie remembered: "Directing the dogfights like Sir John Barbarolli, conductor of the Halle Orchestra". This was the nerve centre of the aircraft, and the aerial director had a communications system which enabled him to speak to the pilots of the Mitchell as well as (via the B-25 crew) to the pilots of the aircraft that were to be filmed. He also sat in front of a bank of television monitors, linked to each of the cameras in the Mitchell, so that he could see the images being captured on film.

The monitors were wired up to videotape machines, which gave an instant playback facility. This, in theory, was an ideal situation as it gave the director the ability to re-shoot the scene during the same aerial sortie, without recourse to landing, re-briefing and taking off again. This could save the Aerial Unit considerable amounts of money, a commodity which became increasingly critical as the filming schedule progressed during the summer of 1968. In practise, this system did not work quite how the film-makers had envisaged it!

By far the most recognisable modification to the B-25 was the nose glazing. The standard framed bomb aimer's position had been removed and was replaced with a specially mounted hemispherical Plexiglas bubble, giving a 180-degree coverage for the Panavision camera mounted inside the nose compartment. Final modification to the aircraft involved a retracting double-jointed arm with a remote-control camera fitted to the end. This arrangement could be lowered out of the bomb bay, with a 360-degree coverage. While this last 'mod' would have undoubtedly captured some spectacular footage, it is not known if it was actually used during the filming. These extensive modifications to the B-25 took three months to complete, at an estimated cost of $75,000.

Complementing all of the sophisticated equipment inside the Mitchell was an exterior paint scheme, which earned the aircraft its nickname of *The Psychedelic Monster*. So that the different formations of Heinkels, Messerschmitts, Hurricanes and Spitfires could easily identify where the aerial director wanted them positioned, the B-25 was painted in a very distinctive set of colours. The forward fuselage and nose were finished in natural metal, with a white section which carried the film logo, plus the legend 'Euramericair associated with Visionair Intnl'. The port side of the bomber's rear fuselage was coloured red; the starboard was painted green. These colours were carried through to the aircraft's twin tail fins. Engine cowlings were white and the remainder of the nacelles were yellow.

Most distinctive of all were the wings, which were painted with a series of black and white chord-wise stripes. While the Mitchell's colour scheme was certainly different, the logic behind the markings worked like a dream. The aircraft was highly visible in the sky, which made it easy for the vintage fighters and bombers to home in on the cameras.

Flying the Mitchell, along with Hawke, for the filming sequences was well-known American warbird pilot Duane Egli. Manning the cameras were two of the world's best aerial cameramen, Skeets Kelly and John Jordan. Sadly, both of these two experts in their field were killed while participating in airborne filming after the *Battle of Britain* had been completed. Kelly died in the mid-air collision of an SE.5A replica and the helicopter cameraship during the filming of the 1971 film *Zeppelin*. John Jordan had earlier diced with death during the shooting of the James Bond film *You Only Live Twice*, in which the lower part of one of his legs was severed by a helicopter rotor blade. During the shooting of the war film *Catch 22* in 1970 Jordan fell out of the rear turret of the B-25 cameraship (N1203). *Battle of Britain* stands as a lasting testament to the airborne camera skills of Kelly and Jordan.

The *Psychedelic Monster* was utilised both in Spain, where it weaved among the mass formations of Messerschmitts and Heinkels, and back in the UK where its cameras captured the bulk of the aerial dogfights. Hawke and Egli managed to put the aircraft exactly where the director wanted it, whether it be slowed right down almost on the point of stall so that large numbers of Heinkels could roar over the top of the camera-equipped tail turret, or guiding the Messerschmitts, Spitfires and Hurricanes up through the UK's bad summer weather in search of some sunshine for the cameras.

Certain guidelines were laid down for the Mitchell's use as a flying camera platform. A Spitfire Productions memo from Director Guy Hamilton, dated March 25, 1968, states:

"B-25 On A Parallel Course With The Planes. There are only two scenes in the film when the formations are riding steadily along prior to engagements by the RAF. No more time than necessary should be devoted to these three or four cuts, because we are after combat material. In every instance, from the RAF viewpoint, combat material will commence with an eye-line of the enemy – either below us or above us and very distant. The B-25 now comes into its own. What will give the material a sense of speed and movement is the closing in rate between the camera and the formation. Wherever possible the camera plane should veer off – bank or turn so as to bring the tail camera into play."

Jeff Hawke and Duane Egli flew the Mitchell for some 300 hours during the filming schedule in order to capture the 40 minutes-worth of spectacular formation and dogfight sequences seen in the final print of the movie.

In late 1969 the bomber, its work on the film completed, returned to the USA, where it lapsed into dereliction at Caldwell Airport, New Jersey.

Group Captain Bader (left) with another technical advisor – namely Squadron Leader James 'Ginger' Lacey, who flew Hurricanes with 501 Squadron and became one of the most successful RAF fighter aces of the Battle of Britain. (*HMP*)

Subject of several legal arguments as to its ownership, the Mitchell was eventually acquired by Atlas Aircraft, who sold it in March 1975 to Ten Plus One Inc. The B-25's sojourn with this owner was short, as in 1977 it was sold to Tom Reilly at Orlando in Florida. By then the Mitchell was in need of total restoration, which Reilly undertook to his usual thorough standard.

Rebuilt to stock B-25J configuration, Tom Reilly operated the bomber on the airshow circuit painted as *Chapter XI*, selling the aircraft to the B-25th Bomber Group Inc at Pompano Beach, Florida, in February 1979. Sold again in 1994 to Dan Powell at Boerne in Texas, the aircraft is now operated as *Lucky Lady* and is in Australia.

Over the years a handful of B-25 Mitchells have been used as aerial camera ships in the UK. N7614C, now on static display inside the American Air Museum at Duxford, was utilised for air to air filming in a British Overseas Airways Corporation promotions film involving a Boeing 747 'Jumbo Jet' during 1970. N9089Z was the camera platform for the film *633 Squadron* in 1964, actually appearing on screen in pseudo RAF markings as an agent-dropping aircraft.

N1042B, a former well-known platform with Tallmantz Aviation in the USA, was flown across the Atlantic in 1988 and used by Aces High Ltd as the camera ship during the filming of the controversial television series *Piece of Cake*. The following year the bomber was used as the main flying camera platform for the cinema production of *Memphis Belle*. It returned to the USA during 1996.

While all of these Mitchells have played an important part in small and large screen epics, N6578D, the *Psychedelic Monster*, was the most modified of the whole bunch and was undoubtedly the one with the most outlandish colour scheme!

Reel 6

Colours and Codes

When it came to painting the vintage aircraft fleet in authentic markings for the film, the producers faced a thorny problem. Should they use squadron codes for the British and German aircraft, which would represent actual units during the Battle of Britain 1940, or should the markings be entirely fictitious? If they used actual codes, then there was no way that every active unit could be represented on both sides, which would inevitably lead to the 'Why wasn't my old squadron shown in the film?' argument.

Faced with this dilemma, Saltzman and Fisz decided to go for the fictitious option, thereby not intentionally upsetting anyone. The film's research team set to work in order to come up with useable squadron code letters and serials, which were believed not to have been issued during the war. This task was not as easy as it sounded, for during wartime there were so many anomalies in terms of the colours and markings set down by the Air Ministry, and what was actually painted on the aircraft 'in the field', it could not be 100% sure that the code combinations picked for the film had not appeared somewhere before between 1939 and 1945.

However, a choice of code letters was decided upon, although all of them would not actually appear in the final print of the film. Spitfires would use AI, BO, CD, DO, EI, EQ and LC squadron codes, with serials in the N2210 to N3445 range. Hurricanes would wear GH, KV, MI, and OQ codes, plus just individual aircraft code letters during the Battle of France scenes, with serials in the H3418 to H3430 range.

There was one exception to this, when Hurricane IIC PZ865 (G-AMAU) wore the authentic markings (OK-I) carried by Keith Park's personal Hurricane, used by the AVM to inspect his squadrons 'in the field' during 1940. This guise was seen in two scenes, when Park arrives unannounced at Canfield's airfield (Hawkinge) and again at Northolt, when Park flies in for the heated meeting with Leigh-Mallory and Dowding.

All of the squadron codes and serials were made by the 3M company in a 'Fablon-style' material, so that they could be changed on a regular basis. This resulted in many aircraft wearing different markings on both sides of the fuselage in order to cut down on the number of aerial filming sorties.

If keeping track of the British aircraft seems difficult, then the German markings have, over the years, proved to be an absolute nightmare. Patchy information on the use of the aircraft in Spain has resulted in little conclusive proof of codes and unit insignia carried by the Messerschmitts and Heinkels. However, it is known that the Heinkels carried 3N, A4, A5, VI, U6 and 6J Staffel codes. The Messerschmitt 109s adopted a coding system of matching the colours of the codes with that worn by the aircraft's propeller spinner, i.e. red codes – red spinner. Throughout the film only three colours were worn, white (used only during the attack on the French airfield sequence), red and yellow. The Messerschmitts also carried Staffel crests on the fuselage below the cockpit, which were changed to match the codes worn. This also applied to the Heinkels. These ever-changing combinations of markings must have been a continuity girl's ultimate headache!

In terms of camouflage colours worn by the film's RAF and Luftwaffe, dark earth/dark green top surfaces with duck egg blue undersides adorned the Hurricanes and Spitfires, while the standard 1940-style two-tone green splinter camouflage with blue undersides was carried by the Heinkels and Messerschmitts. The latter colours helped enormously to disguise the Spanish origins of the movie's Luftwaffe. It was noted that the centre 'Red' of the fuselage roundels on all the Spitfires was reduced in diameter shortly before the start of filming, save for MH415 that had been despatched to Spain.

RAF Code and Serial Combinations
At the time of filming, a number of aviation writers went into print not realising the complexity and the rapidity of change of the film codes and serials applied to the Spitfires and not fully grasping the true identities of the almost identical aircraft. Subsequent writers amalgamated these writings to form a 'list of lists' containing many errors. Spitfire historian Peter Arnold has made a 50-odd year study of the film's Spitfires, accumulating hundreds of images to form an extensive identity data base.

Peter writes that, "Presented here are the analyses of those images. The symbol '*' indicates that the digit in the code/serial is missing, either awaiting application, or is not visible or readable, particularly in the ground to air images. Although upward of a further dozen or more code/serial combinations have been proffered, without a supporting image they have not been included here. Interestingly even the code applicator technician looks to have made the odd error in this continuity nightmare with a Spitfire serial starting with N22** instead of N33**. I am also suspicious of a lone Spitfire briefly carrying the individual code letter V. There is also at least one formation sortie where two Spitfires are carrying the same code letters."

SPITFIRES

Identity   *Code/Serial*

AR213   AI-A, AI-B/N3311, AI-E, AI-G/N3316, AI-H/N3322, AI-N/N3322, BO-E/N3314, CD-B/N3311, CD-C/N3312, CD-H/N3317, CD-K or J/*****, **-R/N3327, EI-E/N3314, EQ-H/*****

P7350   AI-A/N3310, AI-C/N3***, AI-E/N3310, **-S/N3329, BO-C/N3317, BO-H/N3317, CD-B/N3312, CD-C/N3312, CD-D/N331*, CD-E/N3310, CD-G/N3316, CD-H/N3317, CD-M/N3321, DO-E/*****, DO-M/N3321, EI-C/N3312, EI-Q/N3324

AB910   AI-C/N3312, AI-E/N3314, AI-F/N****, AI-H/N3317, AI-J/N3318, AI-M/N3321, AI-N/N****, CD-D/N3313, CD-F/N3315, CD-K/N3319, DO-M/N3321

AR501   AI-C/N3312, AI-E/N3314, AI-G/N3316, AI-H/N3317, AI-J/N3318, AI-L/N3320, BO-B/N3311, BO-H/N3317, CD-D/N3313, CD-F/N3315, CD-J/N3318, CD-K/N3319, CD-V/N3335, DO-A/N3320, DO-G/N3318, DO-H/N3317, EI-C/N3312, EI-Q/N3324

BL614   AI-D/N3313, AI-O/N3327, AI-Q/N3323, BO-D/N3315, BO-F/*****, CD-F or E/*****, CD-Q/N3323, DO-*/*****, DO-N/N3315, EQ-D/N3313

EP120   AI-N/N3312, BO-Q/N3325, DO-*/*****

Colours and Codes   49

MH415   G-AVDJ outward to Spain, and G-AVDJ return to UK,
        AI-A/N2210, AI-C/N3312, AI-D/N331*, AI-E/N3314,
        AI-H/N33**, AI-M/N3321, AI-N/3322, AI-R/*****,
        AI-S/N3329, CD-A/N3310, CD-A/N2210, CD-B/N3311,
        CD-F/N3315, CD-H/N3317, DO-H/N3317, DO-K/N3319,
        DO-M/N3321, EI-G/*****
MH434   AI-A/N3310, AI-D/N3313, AI-E/N3314, AI-G/N3316,
        AI-K/N3319, AI-H/N3317, AI-P/N3324, BO-G/N3316,
        CD-F/N3315, CD-H/N3317, CD-M/N3312, CD-M/N3321,
        DO-H/N3317, DO-L/N3320, DO-N/*****, EI-H/N3317
MJ772   AI-D/N*****, CD-N/*****, CD-H/*****
MK297   AI-A/N3310, AI-B/N3311, AI-H/N3317, AI-M/*****,
        CD-A/N3310, CD-B/N3311, CD-E/N3314, DO-A/*****,
        DO-B/N3311, DO-H/N3317, DO-R/N3327, EI-A/N3313
MK356   AI-R/N3328, BO-H/N3317
TE308   AI-B/*****, AI-E/***20, CD-A/*****, CD-D/***20,
        CD-F/*****, CD-J/*****, CD-K/*****, CD-O/***20,
        DO-H/*****, DO-K/*****, DO-L/*****, DO-S/*****,
        EI-J/*****
RM689   AI-A/N3310, AI-J/N33**, AI-M/N3321, AI-N/N3322,
        AI-O/*****, BO-B/N3311, CD-D/N3313, CD-J/N3318,
        CD-N/*****, DO-D/N3313, DO-M/N3321
RW382   AI-L/*****, AI-G/N3316, AI-H/N3317, BO-E/N****,
        BO-H/N3317, CD-E/N3314, DO-M/N3314, DO-L/N3320,
        DO-U/*****, EQ-G/N3316, EQ-L/N3310
SL574   AI-A/N3310, CD-A/N3310, DO-*/*****, EI-A/N3310
SM411   **-*/N3318, **-S/*****, AI-A/N3310, AI-B/N3311,
        AI-P/N3324, AI-S/N3329, BO-J/*****, CD-E or F/*****,
        DO-R/N3323, EQ-M/N3321, LC-M/N332*
TB382   AI-A/N3310, AI-E/*****, AI-F/*****, AI-G/N3323,
        AI-H/N3317, AI-O/N3327, AI-P/N3324, AI-Q/N3323,
        AI-Q/N3328, AI-R/*****, BO-B/*****, BO-H/N3317,
        CD-A/N3310, CD-B/*****, CD-D/*****, CD-L/N3320,
        DO-A/N3310, DO-L/N3320, DO-M/N3321,
        EQ-A/N3370, LC-A/N3370, **-Q/N3323
TE311   AI-M/N3321, DO-*/N3324, **-M/*****

TE356	AI-C/N3321, AI-H/*****, AI-P/N3324, AI-Q/N3323, AI-R/N3328, BO-C/N*****, CD-C/N3314, DO-C/N3312, DO-P/N3324, LC-C/N3312, LC-L/N3312
TE384	AI-E/N3314, AI-H/N3320, AI-L/N3320, AI-Q/N3323, BO-E/N3314, BO-G/N****, CD-D/*****. DO-E/****. DO-*/N3316, DO-L/N3320, EQ-E/N3314, EQ-F/N3315, LC-F/N3315
TE476	AI-A/N3310, AI-B/N3311, CD-N/N3323, DO-K/*****
PM631	AI-E/N3314, AI-H/N3317, AI-L/N3320, CD-F/N3315, CD-H/*****, CD-K/N3319, DO-G/N3316, DO-N/N3317
PM651	AI-S/N3329, BO-S/N3329
PS853	AI-E/N3314, AI-G/N3316, AI-K/*****, AI-M/N3321, CD-A/*****, CD-C/N3316, CD-K/*****, EI-K/N3319
PS915	AI-R/N3328
LA198	AI-G/N3316, BO-C/N3316

HURRICANES

Identity	Code	Serial
P2617	MI-C, MI-S	H3426, H3427
Z7015	F, L, MI-A, MI-D	H3418
LF363	F, MI-A, MI-D, MI-H, KV-C	H3420, H3421, H3422
LF751	Nil (Replica mould master)	Nil
PZ865	H, MI-C, MI-D, MI-G, KV-A, KV-M, OK-I	H3421, H3423, H3424
RCAF 5377/ G-AWLW	D, F, MI-A, MI-D, MI-F, KV-B	H3418, H3421, H3423

MESSERSCHMITT 109/HISPANO HA 1112 BUCHON

C4K-31 (G-AWHE)	Red 8
C4K-61 (G-AWHF)	Red 8 Ground loop Duxford 21/5/68 not repaired
C4K-75 (G-AWHG)	Yellow 11, Red 14
C4K-99 (G-AWHM)	Yellow 5, Yellow 7
C4K-100 (G-AWHJ)	Red 13, plus MI-V Hurricane codes

C4K-102 (G-AWHK)	Red 7, Yellow 10
C4K-105 (G-AWHH)	Red 4, Red 8, Yellow Chevron & bar
C4K-106 (G-AWHI)	Yellow 4, Yellow 8, plus chevron and bar used Spitfire exhaust stacks
C4K-112 (G-AWHC)	Red 11, Also flew with Yellow Spinner two-seat HA 1112 M4L
C4K-122 (G-AWHL)	Yellow 7, plus MI-T Hurricane codes
C4K-126 (G-AWHD)	Red 9, Yellow 9
C4K-127 (G-AWHO)	White 3, plus MI-S Hurricane codes
C4K-130 (G-AWHN)	Black chevron marks
C4K-144 (G-AWHP)	Red 3
C4K-152 (G-AWHR)	White 5 White 10, plus chevron and gruppe III
C4K-169 (G-AWHT)	Red 5, Yellow 11
C4K-170 (G-AWHS)	Yellow chevron marks

Six Buchons were restored up to taxying status and were used in the Spanish sequences at Tablada and El Corpero. No details are available on the markings carried by airframes C4K-107, C4K-121, C4K-131, C4K-134, C4K-135 and C4K-172. In addition, four Buchons were transported to the UK for use as spares during the English filming sequences. C4K-30, C4K-111, C4K-114 and C4K-154.

Details regarding the markings carried by the Spanish Air Force Heinkel/CASA 2.111 fleet have always been sketchy to say the least, suffice to say that documentary evidence only exists for the two aircraft that came to the UK with the Messerschmitts.

HEINKEL III/CASA 2.111

G-AWHA	6J+BR, 6J+PR, VI+CL, A5+BN
G-AWHB	6J+PR, U6+DL, U6+GN, VI+BN, A5+ER

Reel 7

Model Work

There is no doubt that Hamish Mahaddie had gathered together a formidable array of real aircraft to re-fight the Battle of Britain, but it was obvious that a certain amount of model work would still be needed for the film's extensive aerial dogfight sequences. Aircraft blowing up or crashing into the sea could not be simulated in any other way, apart from in model form. Work with miniatures in previous aviation films had often left something lacking in the credibility department. One only has to look back at productions such as *633 Squadron*, *The Way to the Stars*, *Angels One Five* and *Reach for the Sky*, all of which were let down with the use of dubious-looking and sub-standard models. However, one must also bear in mind the time periods when these earlier films were made. These productions were obviously limited to the technology available at the time of shooting and really should be judged in this context.

Considering that *Battle of Britain* was in production just four years after the 'Airfix-style' Mosquito models were seemingly flying around flat corners in *633 Squadron*, the scale aircraft used in *Battle* had come on in leaps and bounds, as had the handling and filming of them. It was in early 1967 that the decision was taken by *Battle*'s producers to involve the model makers in the film's shooting.

Under the control of John Siddal, who had been responsible for the stunning model work on Stanley Kubrick's *2001 A Space Odyssey*, a team of four distinguished radio control model builders/flyers were gathered together. Mick Charles, Jack Morton, Chris Olsen and David Platt were contracted by Spitfire Productions to put together and fly a 'model air force'. Originally their task was to design and build three prototypes to assess the practicalities of using flying models in the film.

Three main types were chosen when work started at Pinewood Studios on 16 January 1967, the Junkers Ju 87 Stuka, Messerschmitt Bf 110 and Hawker Hurricane. The Stuka was actually modelled on the RAF Museum's late war Ju 87D model, as at that time it was thought that the

Another Battle of Britain ace recruited as a technical advisor was Group Captain Peter Townsend, commander of 85 Squadron during the Battle of Britain. (*HMP*)

real aircraft would be restored to flying condition and used in the aerial sequences. Filming requirements were mapped out and a total of 100 models were deemed necessary for the aerial scenes. This meant that a quick construction method had to be developed by the model makers. Jack Morton devised a moulding process for glass fibre construction, which at that stage was almost unheard of in model making circles.

It was originally planned to have all of the aircraft equipped with retractable undercarriages, but it soon became apparent that this would lead to weight and complexity problems, so a launch trolley system was adopted which proved to be highly successful. Belly landing the models in the grass after filming proved to cause the least damage. With Hamish Mahaddie's negotiations bearing fruit with the Spanish Air Force, the model makers then centred their attentions on the Spitfire, Hurricane, Hispano Buchon and CASA 2.111.

54   Battle of Britain: The Movie

All of the aircraft were constructed to one eighth scale, which was deemed large enough to portray the desired effect on screen, the team were provided with a small workshop at Pinewood Studios, and work started on the model production line. Aerial cameraman Skeets Kelly assessed the models for their ability to be 'mixed in' with the full scale aircraft, which proved to be remarkably good, but on 10 March 1967, the team received a letter from Hugh Attwooll, the film's Production Supervisor, which read: "Due to many factors it does not seem possible that the production of *The Battle of Britain* can proceed. It is with great reluctance therefore, that I must give you the appropriate notice of termination of employment in accordance with your letter of engagement.

Group Captain Townsend and Squadron Leader Lacey with Spitfire. (*HMP*)

Model Work   55

"It is however, possible that, due to the circumstances, we may request an extension of your employment for one or two weeks to assist our endeavours to 'run down' our operations. May I take this opportunity of thanking you all for your assistance on this project and record the appreciation of myself and this Company for all your efforts. Yours Sincerely, for and on behalf of Spitfire Productions Ltd. Hugh Attwooll."

This was indeed a bitter blow for the team, and they all reluctantly went their separate ways.

However, just seven months later the film was back on track with a new financial backer, and the model makers returned to Pinewood. Jack Morton's fast construction method now came into its own, for as is usual in film work, everything was needed yesterday. A special dispensation had been arranged for the models to be able to fly without silencers fitted, which meant that the models could retain a more authentic profile, although the noise of the models flying through the air must have been deafening!

'Weathered' to match the appearance of the real aircraft, the model air force was then ready for the cameras. The Stukas were fitted with small bombs on bomb-release carriers, as used on the real Ju 87s. This meant that a separate radio control transmitter had to be used to make the Stukas release their deadly cargo during the attack on the Ventnor Radar Station scene (the only scene when the model Ju 87s would be used). This second transmitter could also be used to trigger off small explosive charges, which ignited fuel supplies carried in contraceptive condoms inserted inside the model Stukas.

Markings on the models had to be co-ordinated with the real aircraft for any given scene, and this certainly kept the continuity department staff busy. Much of the actual model filming was carried out near Lasham and Duxford, with a large-scale dummy radar station being constructed for the Ventnor scene. This consisted of the upper part of the four radar towers, as the lower portion would be built to full scale for the ground scenes in the film. The two portions would then be edited together in the cutting room after shooting was finished on the film. One memorable scene in the film features a pair of the Ju 87 models colliding in mid-air. This was totally unplanned, but was thankfully captured on film by six cameras. After watching the rushes the film's producers asked the model team to repeat the occurrence with other models, but try as they may it could not be done.

As with the full-size aircraft, the weather interrupted the filming schedule, so much so that the model unit was moved out to Malta in order to secure some blue-sky backdrops in October 1968. This was the last bout of flying for the film models, and with no further use for them, only three of the aircraft actually returned to the UK intact, the rest, their job done, were set on fire in a large bonfire at the Malta location, thus bringing to a close some 21 months of work for the model unit.

Viewed over five decades after they were filmed, the model sequences included in *Battle* still look convincing, despite great strides having subsequently been made in the use of models in films, and the almost taken for granted Computer-Generated Images (CGI) in movies these days. That the model scenes still hold their own is testament indeed to the skills of a small close-knit and talented team who provided a very important part of the filming of *Battle of Britain*.

Reel 8

On Location

Whereas Saltzman and Fisz struck lucky with the numbers of aircraft that could be gathered for the filming, when it came to sourcing authentic-looking airfield locations there were very few that would readily fit the bill. Most surviving airfield locations of the 1940 period were either now housing estates or, if still in use as airfields, had been developed so much that they would prove to be unsuitable for the period look that the producers needed. It was originally estimated that five separate airfields would be needed to convey the RAF

Group Captain Townsend and Spitfire. (*HMP*)

side of the Battle. This was later trimmed down to three main locations, Duxford, Hawkinge and North Weald. Debden Airfield would also be used as an operations base by the flying unit when Duxford was required for ground filming (Henlow, Northolt, Sywell and Panshanger were also used for some limited filming).

1960s starlet Susannah York on set at Duxford in 1968 as a very convincing 'Section Officer Harvey' of the Women's Auxiliary Air Force. (*HMP*)

Negotiations to get permission to use these locations took a long time to come to fruition (*see* Film Logistics), but eventually a deal was secured which meant that the film makers could proceed with the ground-bound sequences in Britain. Of the trio of airfields, Duxford proved to be the most useful, as it actually portrayed different locations in the finished film, the French airfield which was constructed on the south-west corner of Duxford, the main airfield and its hangars portrayed the station commanded by Kenneth More.

The 'South Downs Flying Club' (where Michael Caine and his squadron are evacuated to after 'Hawkinge' is put out of action) was for many years associated with Duxford, but it was actually filmed at RAF Henlow centred around the original Watch Office.

One of the main stations in the real Battle, Duxford had lain unused since the RAF moved out in August 1961. Since then the airfield had been under Care and Maintenance, but basically remained unchanged from its wartime vista, save for the hard runway, which was built in 1951 to accommodate jet fighters. After the film company moved out there were several suggestions put forward for the future use of Duxford, one of them being that the site should be converted into an open prison!

Thankfully the latter never came to pass. During the mid-1970s the London-based Imperial War Museum (IWM) used the airfield as a storage facility for some of its larger aircraft exhibits. This idea gained momentum and the airfield eventually became a fully-fledged arm of the IWM, which along with support from the Duxford Aviation Society, opened the complex to the public. Over the years the museum has gone from strength to strength and today ranks as the leading centre for historic aircraft preservation in Europe (some say the world!). Apart from the IWM's impressive collection of static aircraft, Duxford is home to an ever-increasing number of airworthy warbirds, operated by a host of private owners.

Over the years Duxford has grown into one of Britain's major aviation attractions, and although some may say that the airfield has lost its authentic wartime feel with the modern-looking 'Superhangar' and American Air Museum, it remains a magnet to anyone who has an interest in historic aviation. The house occupied by Sqn Ldr Skipper (Robert Shaw) in the film is located in Sawston Village north of Duxford, proving

Susannah York in a powerful scene following the bombing of Duxford – sadly York died in 2011, aged 72. (*HMP*)

that filmatic licence came into play yet again, as Skipper was supposedly based at North Weald!

North Weald Airfield in Essex, like Duxford, had a genuine Battle of Britain history and apart from a jet extension to the main runway still retained that 'wartime look' so needed by the film producers. Weald was transferred to the Army in 1966 and was also being used as a gliding centre, but for filming purposes little had to be done to turn it back to a wartime Fighter Command airfield. The modern control tower was covered with camouflage netting and one of the T2 hangars was given a wartime hue. Dispersal huts and various other airfield buildings were hastily constructed on the northern side of the airfield, in front of the remaining wartime revetments and row of Poplar trees, the latter still giving North Weald its unmistakable 'signature' today.

In recent years North Weald has become home to an increasing number of historic aircraft. The fully restored and 'operational' wartime-style buildings that formed *The Squadron* are now owned by the Aero Legends organisation. They represent the airfield's wartime image and in effect keep the 1939-45 spirit of the airfield alive, while visitors who wish to learn more of this famous site can do no better than to make a visit to the North Weald Airfield Museum, housed in the former station office at the original entrance to the airfield.

Hawkinge, the third of the film's major external locations, was at the time of filming still an all-grass airfield, and in that respect was the most authentic of all the venues used. Officially closed down in December 1961, by the time the film makers got around to using the airfield it was bereft of any buildings whatsoever, so dispersal huts, and dummy hangars had to be constructed by Spitfire Productions in order to achieve the correct image for the film. While the dispersal areas could boast proper three-dimensional facilities, the hangars on the far side of the airfield were in effect 'flat' lookalikes, held up by a copious amount of scaffolding. Viewed close-up the effect was not very convincing, but seen in long shot in the final film it is difficult to tell that the hangars are not real.

Today, Hawkinge holds perhaps the largest number of *Battle of Britain* film reminders, for the Kent Battle of Britain Museum has CASA 2111 B21-103 and a number of the replica Hurricanes, Spitfires and Messerschmitts built for the movie on display. All have been restored and are kept in fine condition. Testament indeed to the high standard of their original construction back in 1968.

As to the film's non-airfield locations in the UK, there were the extensive London Blitz scenes, which would be needed to be represented if the complete story of the Battle was to be depicted. In this area the film company struck gold, for in 1967 and 1968 the Greater London Council

Pilots scramble for their Hurricanes in 'France' – Duxford, 1968. (*GBC*)

(GLC) was in the process of carrying out a slum clearance plan. The old 1930s and 1940s terraced houses of London's east end were being torn down to make way for the planned high-rise flats. Spitfire Productions must have seemed like manner from heaven to the GLC, for they wanted to 'borrow' a couple of streets, plus some warehouses in the St Katherine's Dock area of the city and blow them up for the cameras. In effect the film company wanted to do the council's job for them and pay them for the privilege!

Dragon Road, just off the Camberwell Road, in London's SE.15, was chosen, and in early May the film's special effects experts, Cliff Richardson and Glen Robinson, moved in and rigged the street with a series of high explosive charges. By this time the vast majority of occupants had moved out and been found new accommodation by the GLC, but there were still a couple of families in residence, who, having lived through the original Blitz and survived were determined not to be moved by a film company wanting to re-create the night raids on London for the cinema. Spitfire Productions therefore had to compensate them for the inconvenience and ensure that their houses were properly safeguarded with piles of sandbags!

On the night of 9 May 1968, Dragon Road was demolished for the Panavision cameras. Lorry loads of car windscreens were smashed up and piles of bricks and rubble were littered around the 'set' to create the devastation needed for the correct effect. By 4.30am the following morning the shooting was finished and the whole mess created for the cameras had to be cleared up so that the GLC could carry on with the development of the area. The following night the effects team set their sights on St Katherine's Dock, where an old tea warehouse 'bit the dust' for the cameras.

Even London's famous Underground train system did not escape the attention of the film company. One night, after the trains had stopped running, Aldwych Station, which is situated on a spur off the Piccadilly Line, was 'dressed' for its part in *Battle of Britain*. Posters advertising the latest films and shows in London were covered over with wartime designs, 'Careless Talk Costs Lives', Churchill's 'Let Us Go Forward Together' etc. Many Londoners who, as children, had lived through the real blitz were employed as 'extras' for the scenes in the 'Tube Station'.

The scene where Archie, played by Edward Fox, parachutes into the rear garden of a suburban house before being offered a cigarette by a young schoolboy, was actually one of the last location scenes filmed. This was shot in Ealing, West London, in November 1968, and required Edward Fox to be lowered into the garden while attached to a parachute style harness suspended from a crane parked in the street nearby.

Other filming locations seen briefly included Saffron Waldon where the rear courtyard of a premises in Market Lane was used for a shot of the 'Prize Bakery Chilham' sign preceding Maggie's introduction to 'Squadron Leader Tom Evans' played by W.G. Foxley.

One other location lingers in the memory of those who are keen *Battle of Britain* film enthusiasts, that being the Jackdaw Inn, where Sqn Ldr Colin Harvey, played by Christopher Plummer, ordered a 'large scotch' for the princely sum of 'one and six'. This public house still exists and for many years the exterior was little changed from its persona on screen. However, a recent re-vamp has sadly seen it lose its film 'look'. The Jackdaw is located on the A260 road at Denton, near Canterbury, in Kent.

One ground location, which played itself in the film, was Bentley Priory, near Stanmore in Middlesex. Home to Air Chief Marshal Dowding's Fighter Command Headquarters, it was obvious that this significant building would have to be portrayed at some stage in the production. While all the internal scenes, Dowding's office and the Operations Room, were re-created at Pinewood Film Studios, the external sequences were shot in the grounds of the Priory itself, including the final scene where Laurence Olivier (as Dowding) walks out onto the balcony while the end titles roll up the screen.

When RAF Fighter Command was formed in 1936, its headquarters was moved into Bentley Priory and extensive work was started in early 1939 to prepare the building for the onslaught of war. The excavation needed to construct the underground operations centre required the

'German bomber crews' awaiting inspection. (*GBC*)

removal of some 58,000 tons of earth before the 17,000 tons of reinforced concrete could be poured in to create the whole complex.

Declared operational in March 1940 (just in time for the Battle), it was from here that Dowding took the vitally important decisions regarding the disposition of his squadrons in the thick of the fighting. Still in RAF control, Bentley Priory must rank as one of the air force's most historic buildings as the tactics decided upon within its walls undoubtedly saved this country from invasion in 1940. The first sequence in the film, that of a lone Hurricane performing a victory roll over the heads of the retreating British Army in France, was actually filmed in the country roads adjacent to Pinewood Film Studios, while the film's Ventnor Radar Station (supposedly on the Isle of Wight) and the Observer Corps post were located on ground known as 'The Mound', near Dover.

The tense meeting at the British Embassy in Switzerland between Baron Von Richter played by Curt Jurgens and Sir David Kelly, played by Sir Ralph Richardson, used an exterior shot filmed at the Municipal Offices of Interlaken in the Bernese Oberland region of Switzerland, while the interior confrontation was filmed at Hall Barn House, Beaconsfield.

Over in Spain the film company made use of a number of different locations. The town of San Sebastian, in northern Spain, was found to include a number of streets which with the right 'dressing' could be made to resemble Berlin in 1940. Along the Avendia de Espana false shop fronts were moved into position, German underground signs, a Police obelisk, newspaper kiosk (complete with 1940 German newspapers), cylindrical advertising drums with period posters in place and the obligatory Nazi flags completed the transformation, and for several nights wartime Berlin was recreated for scenes depicting the RAF attacks on the German capital.

Tablada Airfield was the main operating base for the flying unit, and it was here that the famous opening credits sequence was filmed, using the rows of Heinkel bombers and arriving Junkers Ju 52. Tablada was also disguised to resemble Staken Airport, for the scene in the film when the Heinkel bomber pilots are told to report to Berlin. Sadly, Tablada Airfield is no more, and to add insult to injury a main road now runs through what used to be the middle of the airfield.

El Corpero Airfield, which adjoined Tablada, was the main Messerschmitt 109 base in the film and a corner of this location was used for the scene in which Major Falke (Manfred Reddeman) returns from

Spitfire! (*GBC*)

shooting down Pilot Officer Charlie Lambert. Obviously, both Tablada and El Corpero were supposed to be Luftwaffe forward operating airfields in northern France, so certain measures had to be taken to disguise their Spanish looks.

Hangars were camouflaged, modern buildings were disguised, sentry boxes were built, period vehicles were strategically positioned in front of modern airfield fittings, and, getting right down to the 'nitty gritty', it was also stipulated that a quantity of foliage had to be positioned to cover cactus plants. One doesn't find cactus plants in northern France! The attention to detail in the film's well-known title sequence at Tablada is indicative of the efforts that went in to make this movie as authentic as was possible, 'dressing' requirements for this portion alone were, to say the least, immense!

Two black 'official' cars would be needed for the actors playing the inspecting officers (Milch etc) and one Luftwaffe staff car. All three vehicles would be suitably marked up with registration letters and officers' pennants. The Junkers Ju 52, coded 4Z+JH, would taxi into shot, Milch would disembark and the camera would pan back to show 18 Heinkel bombers lined up in two rows (wearing unit codes on one side only), with attendant crews stationed in front for inspection as Milch was driven past. In the background of the shot several vehicles and pieces of airfield equipment would be positioned to complete the required effect. "Thankfully we did not have to make many alterations to the Junkers 52 for this scene", remembered Hamish Mahaddie. "All we had to do was to camouflage it and remove the chintz curtains from the windows. I don't think that Milch would have liked the chintz curtains."

Four Kubelwagons and eight lorries of suitable vintage had to be found, hired and utilised in this portion of the opening title sequence alone. 20 bomb trolleys, 70 50kg bombs, 30 250kg bombs, two 88mm guns along with their revetments, three light anti-aircraft guns and revetments, plus a wind sock all had to be sourced or specially made.

For the second portion of the title credits the inspecting officers were driven to the adjoining airfield (actually another corner of Tablada Airfield) and, as the procession exits one airfield, four Heinkel 111s had to be moved from the large line-up, re-coded and positioned 'in shot'. Two sentry boxes, an exit barrier along with appropriate signboards were made for the 'shot'.

It has to be said that this level of 'attention to detail, for what amounted to a three-minute sequence in the film, sums up the painstaking determination of the film makers to 'get it right'. Sadly, this level of dedication was lost on the average cinema audience and was only really appreciated by the aircraft enthusiasts who saw the film. That said, *Battle of Britain* would have been a much poorer production if the producers and director had not insisted that the only way to make this film was to do it properly! It is this, which has given the movie its lasting appeal with aviation aficionados.

Reel 9

Summer 1968

While the aerial unit was shooting the Spanish sequences, director Guy Hamilton was having a fleet of replica Spitfires and Hurricanes built in readiness for the film's airfield attack scenes in the UK. Even though some 27 real Spitfires were available for the cameras, it was deemed that this was not enough if the airfields were to look fully 'inhabited' and convincing. This lack of aircraft problem was even more critical with Hurricanes, as only six were available and many more would be needed if RAF Fighter Command of 1940 were to be convincingly portrayed.

'Heinkel'! (*GBC*)

Hispano *Buchon* C4K-152 (G-AWHR) at Tablada. (*GBC*)

Therefore, a temporary factory was set up in three purpose-built tents measuring 120ft by 80ft. Inside the factory, supervisor Ken Softly and his construction team set about building Hurricane, Spitfire and even Me 109 fighters, using moulds cast from Spitfire V BM597, Hurricane IIC LF751 and one of the Henlow Buchons. A good number of these replicas would meet a fiery end during the film's bombing scenes. Most were pure static facsimiles, but some were fitted with motorcycle engines to turn the propellers, it is not known why full scale Buchons were ever manufactured, as they appear to have never been used. These examples would be towed by wires into bomb craters or exploded while 'taxying' on screen. Ken and his crew even produced a full-size CASA 2.111 fuselage, used in the Heinkel crash scene, in which the crew is being rescued after a belly landing back in France. This sequence is reported to have been shot in the fields at the back of Pinewood Film Studios.

Considering that the replica aircraft were built for the purpose of being blown up or wrecked in the film's attack scenes, they were highly detailed, which in terms of authenticity on screen was highly commendable, but this attention to detail by Ken and the rest of the construction crew caused a number of other problems never originally envisaged by the film-makers. When the airfields at Duxford, Hawkinge and North Weald were dressed with a host of real and replica Spitfires, it was sometimes difficult to tell the difference. On several occasions pilots and groundcrews had approached the wrong aircraft, mistaking a *Mark Addie* or replica for an airworthy aircraft, which to say the least was embarrassing for all concerned.

These instances led to some of the RAF contingent issuing an unofficial set of 'Pilots Notes', which were rapidly circulated around all those on the 'set' with a sense of humour:

The Spitfire Mk.68

Description and Identification
The Spitfire Mk.68 is an elliptical winged, single engined aircraft but beyond this, description and identification becomes a little difficult. The Spitfire is normally powered by a Rolls-Royce Merlin, but some Mk. 68 variants are fitted with a 3 horsepower (hp) single cylinder engine usually filched from an unsuspecting lawn mower. (Note: Mk.68 aircraft are easily identified by their three bladed, zero thrust propellers, and also the fact that they are made of fibreglass. Rumours that these aircraft are

'Yellow 13' in Spain. (*GBC*)

From left: Michael Caine (Squadron Leader Canfield), technical advsor and Battle of Britain ace Wing Commander Robert Stanford Tuck, Producer Ben Fisz and Director Guy Hamilton discussing a scene at Hawkinge, 1968. (*GBC*)

made by Airfix and can be bought as kits from Woolworth's, price 6/11d – engine extra – are entirely discounted).

Pre Mk.68 Spitfires can be divided into three main types, flyers, taxiers and ornaments. Unfortunately, they are not easily distinguishable, except in the case of the taxiers which are attempted to be flown, lateral stability being noted to be sadly lacking, due to the fact that the ailerons are not connected up.

Identification by markings is rendered impossible by a group of highly skilled and enthusiastic painters employed by the company, who insist on altering all aircraft markings and letters after each sortie.

Replica Hurricanes dressed for the 'French airfield' attack scene. (*GBC*)

Starting the Engine
The engine may – or may not – start. Failure to start is usually due to mis-identification (see previous paragraph), but may also be due to a variety of other reasons. A positive engine start can normally be ascertained by any of the following symptoms:

1: A small or even large fire burning in the exhaust, or anywhere else for that matter.
2: Groundcrew lying in wounded or maimed attitudes around the aircraft.
3: Aircraft pitches over onto its nose (Engine should normally stop if this occurs, so repeat starting procedure).
4: Crash tender seen leaving for tea-break (normally in association with symptoms mentioned above).

R/T Equipment
The aircraft is fitted with VHF radio and also a locally fitted substitute. On No Account use the aircraft's VHF equipment, as its secondary function is to act as a rear fuselage heater; however the heater function does not use a smokeless fuel and the cockpit will, like as not, fill with thick fumes and smoke, which contravenes the Clean Air Act. Communication with ATC is best accompanied by letter or post-card, but if you feel you must talk to SATCO, always go through Radio Rentals Ltd.

Ancillaries
The Spitfire Mk.68 is fitted with many ancillary devices designed to promote the health, comfort and convenience of the pilot. Take for instance the 'canteen substitute' device fitted to the engine. Pilots may have noticed copious amounts of steam issuing from the side of the engine very shortly after start-up. Wise pilots will have a quarter pound of tea placed in the radiator before start-up, thus ensuring a nice hot cuppa in the event of a force landing, which is quite likely. The steam can also be used to cook edible roots or to take an instant Turkish Bath, whichever the situation may warrant.

Conclusion
The Spitfire Mk. 68 is a remarkable aircraft in all respects. It is a joy to fly, and an even greater joy to land. Treat it badly and it will treat you in a like manner, but treat it with the respect it deserves and, in all probability, it will finish you off altogether!

* * *

One 'real' aircraft type, which was almost extinct, but would have to be portrayed in the film, was the Junkers Ju 87, Germany's infamous Stuka dive-bomber. Stukas were used by the Luftwaffe in the first phase of the Battle, during the attacks on Britain's radar stations. This aircraft type would have to make an appearance in the film if the whole story of the Battle was to be accurately depicted. Spitfire Productions only had one Stuka on strength, that being Ju 87D-5 w/nr 494083, which was on loan from the Ministry of Defence. The MoD at first refused permission for the film company to restore this aircraft to flying condition, although it is believed that Simpson's Aero Services engineers actually managed to get the engine running on one occasion.

Another avenue would have to be explored in order to get Stukas into the film. Once again Vivian Bellamy's expertise in replica building was called upon.

"We had this idea of converting a Percival Proctor into a sort of one-third scale Stuka," recalled Vivian in 1997. "I bought three complete Proctors, plus a dismantled airframe for spares and converted two into Stuka lookalikes. By altering the fuselage, taking out the four-seat cabin, and making the glasshouse-style cockpit canopy to fit what we had left, we had a basic Stuka-looking fuselage. I then took the wings off and altered the centre-section of the wing to resemble the inverted gull-wing configuration, which the Stuka was well known for.

"The un-altered outer wing sections were then bolted back onto the centre section. We put a larger engine in the airframe, and modified the fin, rudder and tailplane to have that angular look. I thought that with the bigger engine and the larger control surfaces at the rear of the aircraft, it should fly pretty well, but in reality, it was bloody awful. The one aircraft, which we actually flew for around five hours before the project got the chop, wallowed about all the time, and we could not actually carry out the near vertical dives which were the trademark of the Ju 87. In reality we could have carried out the dives, but the wings would have come off when we pulled up after releasing the bombs, which was hardly a practical proposition at all. So my scale Stuka was not used. Instead the film company had some large-scale radio-controlled models built and they were used in the final film."

As time went on the Ministry of Defence realised that Spitfire Productions could safely operate the fleet of vintage aircraft in their control, and permission is reported to have eventually been granted to restore the real Stuka to flying condition. Sadly, this revelation came too late for the film, as it would have taken up far too much money to instigate the restoration of the Ju 87, and it would never have been ready in time to meet the filming schedule, so the Stuka remained on the ground.

"God's teeth, take cover!"
Kenneth More

Spitfire warming up ready for more filming. (*GBC*)

While preparations were being made to welcome the aerial unit back from Spain, there was much to be done behind the scenes. John Wilson Apperson, the film's wardrobe manager, was in the process of having up to 2,000 costumes made for the actors and actresses to wear. Ron Baker, one of the production's props men managed to acquire a dozen Spitfire and Hurricane gunsights and a stock of Spitfire main wheels. A security company was contracted to carry out guard duties at the film's main airfield locations, in the expectation of many hundreds of onlookers, who could not only endanger themselves during the forthcoming bombing scenes, but could actually get in the way of air-to-ground photography.

With the large numbers of vintage aircraft being employed in the film, it was obvious that a support organisation would be a major requirement in keeping all of the fighters and bombers serviceable. While John 'Tubby' Simpson and his engineers would, with the benefit of hindsight, work absolute wonders, a consortium of companies from Britain's aircraft industry was seconded for extra back-up. Indeed, a large-scale technical team had been built up to co-ordinate and oversee the production, as well as a number of British and German technical advisors.

"I was in effect a Bomber Baron", remembered Hamish Mahaddie in 1988. "I spent all of my war in RAF Bomber Command, so I felt it was not right that I was the only technical advisor on *Battle of Britain*. I brought in some of the RAF's fighter aces from 1940 so that they could watch the filming and advise if things were not being carried out correctly. People like Wing Commander Robert Stanford Tuck and Squadron Leader 'Ginger' Lacey were invaluable, because they knew what Fighter

Some idea of the equipment required for filming back in 1968! (*GBC*)

The B-25 filming the attack on north-east England scene. (*GBC*)

Command was like in 1940, and were therefore able to keep a wary eye on what went into the cameras each day.

"We didn't have many real problems because the producers and director had done their homework well, but we did, from time to time, have trouble with some of the less famous actors who were in the film. People like Laurence Olivier and Michael Caine were fine, but the younger up-and-coming actors sometimes got delusions of grandeur.

"I remember one of them saying that he was not happy about wearing the pilot's oxygen mask, as 'his public' would not be able to recognise him in the cockpit scenes. So Ginger Lacey said to him one day 'Look, you see that film extra stood over there, well he will be more than happy to wear the mask and swap his £25 per day for your £250 per day'. From that day on we had no more trouble with the 'bit players'. Ginger Lacey was very effective in what he did on the film."

The Battle of Britain Technical Advisory Team

Chief Technical Advisor:	G/C T.G. Mahaddie DSO DFC AFC C.Eng, AFRaeS
Deputy:	W/C C.G. St Jeffries DFC
Ministry of Defence (RAF) Policy:	A.B. Twist (DPR Dept)
RAF Project Officer:	W/C C.G. St Jeffries

Tactical

Tactical Advisor RAF:	W/C R.R. Stanford Tuck DSO DFC
Deputy:	S/L J. Lacey DFM
Research, Air Historical Branch:	L.A. Jackets
Radar:	W/C M.G. Lovell RAF HQ Fighter Command
Plotting (WAAF):	W/C C. Legge WAAF HQ Fighter Command
Tactical Advisor (Luftwaffe):	General A. Galland
Deputy:	Oberst H. Brustellin
Aero Engineering (Manager):	F/L R.G. Boorman RAF Henlow
Simpsons Aero Services:	John Simpson
Field Support Consortium:	Rolls-Royce
Dowty-Rotol	
Smiths Aerospace	
KLG Plugs	
Dunlop	
British Oxygen	
Delaney Galley	
Triplex	
Lucas	
Cellon	
Military Air Traffic Organisation:	W/C L.C. Young (RAF)
Arnold Field (CAA)	

Air Registration Board

Aircraft Importation & Re-export: P. Whitcher

	Aircraft Entry Carnet
Royal Aero Club:	J. Blake
Customs Advisor:	J.G. Lambie

	Madrid
British Embassy: (Air Attaché)	G/C R. Coulson
Spitfire Production Office:	Agustin Pastor
Malaga:	Lt Col D. Antonia Rivas Monroe
Tablada:	Cmdt Col J.M.A. Del Valle Rodriguez
Officer i/c Maintenance:	Capt Francisco Sanchez Collado
Chief Test Pilot (Bf 109s):	Cmdt Pedro Santa Cruz

During the time while the aerial unit were in Spain, the film's major stars, in the human sense of the word, were being called up for duty and were in the studios filming the interior scenes for the movie. The interiors

Spitfire PR.XIX PM631 of the Battle of Britain Flight. (*GBC*)

80 Battle of Britain: The Movie

were a mixture of real locations and recreations; the latter specially built at Pinewood. The early pre-credits scene in the film, where Dowding (Sir Laurence Olivier) walks down the long passage en-route to the lift which serves Sir Francis Stokes' (Harry Andrews) office, was shot in the Ministry of Defence buildings in Whitehall, London. The lift attendant was played by 69-year-old Edward Williams, a role he took in real life. This short scene was filmed on a quiet Sunday morning, so that the film crew would not disturb the workings of the 'powers that be' at Whitehall in their day to day tasks.

Other interiors had to be painstakingly re-created for the cameras. Air Chief Marshal Dowding's office at Bentley Priory was pieced together

RAF pilots await the next scramble… maybe their last…. (*GBC*)

at Pinewood, using period photographs and the help of Dowding's one-time right-hand man, Robert Wright. Air Vice-Marshal Keith Park's (Trevor Howard) main operations room was another which had to be built especially for the production. Some of the actors with smaller roles (Nigel Patrick, Sir Michael Redgrave etc) were able to complete their scenes for the film in a matter of days, whereas the more major players were involved for a lot longer, especially those who had airfield sequences as well as interior scenes to film.

> **"Don't just stand there, get one up."**
> *Robert Shaw*

Before the flying unit arrived back in Britain from Spain, negotiations were being carried out between the film company and the UK's air traffic control services. To film the aerial dogfights for *Battle of Britain* it would require sizeable slices of airspace, which for safety reasons would have to be kept clear of other aircraft. Wing Commander Leslie Young, a senior RAF air traffic controller, was seconded to Spitfire Productions by the Ministry of Defence, and it was his task to oversee the flying operations and co-ordinate airspace requirements.

In an unprecedented move, three corridors of the sky above East Anglia and the Midlands were allocated to the film company by the Military Air Traffic Organisation for the duration of shooting. Each of these measured 50 miles long by ten miles wide. NOTAMS (Notices to Airmen) were issued when filming was to take place which in effect cleared these corridors of any unwanted aircraft.

The Royal Air Force agreed to provide a number of pilots to fly the Hurricanes and Spitfires during filming, and, as one could imagine, when this news broke there were lots of eager pilots clamouring to get their names down on the list. From those that applied a final list of ten was drawn up, all of which were Qualified Flying Instructors, with fighter backgrounds. Led by Wing Commander George Elliot from HQ Flying Training Command (who personally selected the pilots by giving them a one-hour flight in one of the Spitfire Tr.9s to see if they could safely handle the aircraft), the rest of the 'lucky ones' included: Sqn Ldr M.A. Vickers – RAF Valley, Sqn Ldr S. St J. Homer – Edinburgh University Air Squadron, Sqn Ldr D.J. Spink – RAF Acklington, Sqn Ldr D.W.

Buchon C4K-31 (G-AWHE) 'Red 8', looking menacing. (*GBC*)

Mills – RAF Cranwell, Flt Lt M.R. Merrett – RAF Linton-on-Ouse, Flt Lt D.J. Curry – RAF Manby, Flt Lt R.D. Coles – RAF Little Rissington, Flt Lt R.B. Lloyd – RAF Little Rissington and Flt Lt J.M. Preece – RAF Oakington.

At the end of the Spanish filming a roster was drawn up at Tablada as to which pilots would be flying the Messerschmitt 109s for the British sequences. The following Spanish Air Force pilots were granted limited periods of leave of absence from their military duties: Pedro Santa Cruz Barcelo, Ramon Guiterrez Martinez, Jose Manuel Alvarez Coterillo, Eladio Ramos Gutierre, Jose Mingot Garcia, Fernando De Artega Danvilla, Jose Antonio Garcia Perez, Julio Arrabal Teran, Jesus Fernandez Trujillo, Carlos Diego Garcia-Bermudez, Fortunato Lanzaron Olmos, Francisco Alvarez Redono, Manuel Cabello Arcas, Francisco Meseguer Garcia, Camillo Vazquez Herjas and Pedro Nieto Matrinez. Wilson 'Connie' Edwards, from the Confederate Air Force in Texas, and Vivian Bellamy in England would accompany these pilots for the flight to England.

May 14, 1968 dawned cold and windy. It was hardly good conditions to welcome the flying unit from Spain. The Heinkels, Messerschmitts, Spitfire and Mitchell had taken five days to fly from Tablada to Duxford, initially landing at RAF Manston in Kent to clear customs, and if this was the sort of weather the film unit would have to put up with in the UK, then things did not look too good for keeping the production on schedule. One Heinkel and a Messerschmitt were stuck in Jersey after suffering taxying accidents on landing, but the rest of the fleet made it to Duxford, after some confusion which saw the formation orbiting over the City of Cambridge. A Spitfire and Hurricane from the RAF's Battle of Britain Flight at Coltishall, plus one of the film's two-seat Spitfires, had

The mock-up He 111 cockpit under construction. (*GBC*)

earlier launched out of Duxford in order to welcome the 'Luftwaffe' to Britain, which was indeed a portent of things to come.

With a strong crosswind that day at Duxford, there were a few dodgy moments as the tired pilots brought their aircraft in to land, but all got down safely and were battened down for the night in readiness for the aerial dogfights to come.

> "Don't you yell at me, Mister Warwick."
> *Susannah York*

As with the Spanish shooting, the film unit was dogged with bad weather in England during the summer of 1968. During late May the French airfield scenes were being shot at the south-western end of Duxford, where the film company had built an impressive-looking chateau. Tents, vehicles and ancillary equipment surrounded this façade, completing the illusion of an Allied Expeditionary Force airfield in northern France at the time of Dunkirk.

While the ground scenes were relatively easy to put 'into the can' the schedule was delayed when it came to filming the Hurricanes taking off. The rain had rendered the grass area on that side of Duxford Airfield unusable and this meant several days of waiting around for the grass to dry before any filming could take place. This scenario of the filming schedule being dictated by the weather conditions had a critical effect on the film's finances, and on more than one occasion Harry Saltzman had to fly out to United Artists in the USA in order to negotiate extra cash for the production.

Almost every day, the pilots, groundcrews, cameramen, and all the other technical personnel needed to operate the vintage aircraft fleet would arrive for briefing at 8am, the sorties of the day would be planned and agreed, the aircraft would be warmed up, only to have the clouds roll in and put a stop to any flying activities for the whole day. This happened time and time again during May, June and July.

The days when the weather was set fair, it was a 'maximum effort' to get as much aerial footage filmed as was humanly possible. Duxford Airfield came alive as the Spitfires, Hurricanes, Messerschmitts and Heinkels, plus the B-25, got airborne and headed off over East Anglia for the filming corridors in the sky. Around an hour later they would all

A Spitfire overtakes a formation of He 111s after an astern attack. (*GBC*)

return and the sortie would be debriefed. Sometimes during the evening, the previous day's footage, the 'rushes', as they are known in the film industry, would be viewed by the director, producers and pilots over in Duxford's former camp cinema.

"Luckily, we managed to attain a fairly good aircraft serviceability record during filming," recalled Hamish Mahaddie. "I originally had allowed for one aircraft to be lost each week, and at the end of the filming schedule we would have no aircraft left. But due to the sheer hard work and determination by Tubby Simpson and his engineers we kept the fleet going right up to the end.

"We had very few real spares we could turn our hands to, so if for instance we had a radiator problem, Tubby would whip it off the aircraft and tear off to Delaney Galley, the radiator specialists, who would fix it overnight, and the radiator would be back on the aircraft by late morning the following day. Trouble was, Tubby was the sort of person who could not really delegate work, and he ended up doing most of it himself. He sadly died shortly after we had finished the film and I'm sure that it was due to the very high workload shouldered by him in keeping all the aircraft flying."

The unenviable task of keeping all of the aircraft under control on the ground and in the air at Duxford fell to Squadron Leader Ron Chadwick. It was his job to see that the laws of the air were obeyed at all times, and it was no mean feat to cope with the vagaries of some 30-plus vintage aircraft on a day to day basis. On the grounds of safety, no low-level beat ups were authorised, although some did inevitably take place by some of the more exuberant pilots when they returned from filming sorties.

The British Board of Trade had issued the Messerschmitts and Heinkels with restricted permits to fly, which enabled them to get airborne for the purposes of aerial filming and moving location only. With the exception of the aircraft operated by the RAF's Battle of Britain Flight, this meant that the film's aircraft fleet was not allowed to take part in any air displays during the months of production.

He 111 G-AWHA belching smoke after landing at Duxford following being 'badly shot up'. (*GBC*)

A Hispano HA112 M1L *Buchon* masquering as a Messerschmitt 109, Yellow 13, fresh from the paint shop at Tablada, Span. (*Gary Brown Collection [hereafter acknowledged as 'GBC']*).

Jack Morton, one of the film's model-makers with flying-scale Spitfires. (*Peter Arnold Collection [hereafter acknowledged as PAC]*).

The flying models used in the film being reassembled in Malta after shipment from England. (*PAC*)

Model Stukas being made ready for the Ventnor Radar Station attack scene – the mock radar pylons can be seen in the background. (*PAC*)

After use in Malta, their 'Duty Carried Out', the majority of models were destroyed to save on return shipping costs. (*PAC*)

Wheeled trolleys used to get the models airborne. (*PAC*)

The *Jackdaw Inn* at Denton, Kent, the exterior of which was used for the scene in which 'Squadron Leader Harvey' (Christopher Plummer) arrives in his green MG as the local Home Guard are falling out in the car park. A must-visit when in the area, as is the nearby Kent Battle of Britain Museum at Hawkinge. (*PAC*)

One of the film's Hurricanes 'on patrol'. (*PAC*)

Hurricane replicas at Duxford ready for the airfield attack sequence during the Battle of France scene. (*PAC*)

'Air Vice-Marshal Park' (Trevor Howard) arrives at 'Squadron Leader Canfields' (Michael Caine) airfield; director Guy Hamilton is wearing the white hat. (*PAC*)

Jack Morton of the film's Model Unit with one of the large-scale flying Hispano *Buchons* used in the movie. (*PAC*)

A CASA2.111 representing a Heinkel 111, pictured at Duxford. (*PAC*)

Hawker Hurricane LF653 representing an aircraft of 303 (Polish) Squadron (the codes of which were actually RF). (*PAC*)

The sole surviving airworthy two-seater Hispano *Buchon* C4K-112 (G-AWHC) was used as a camera-ship during the filming. (*PAC*)

Six Spitfires and a Hurricane preparing to take-off from Duxford during the filming in summer 1968. (*PAC*)

Models being prepared for flight and filming in Malta. (*PAC*)

'Psychedelic Monster' – the B-25 Mitchell camera-ship flown by Jeff Hawke pictured at Duxford, 1968. (*PAC*)

'Me 109 Red 11' taking off from Duxford, 1968n. (*PAC*)

Some of the film's aircraft on the track at Duxford, 1968. (*PAC*)

Filming a scene with 'Squadron Leader Canfield' (Michael Caine). (*PAC*)

The Battle of Britain Flight's Spitfire PRXIX PS853 dressed for filming and pictured en route to display at an airshow in 1968. (*PAC*)

With one engine shut down and trailing 'smoke', simulating damage, a 'He 111' (G-AWHA) snapped low over Duxford. (*PAC*)

The B-25 camera-ship takes-off for another sortie. (*PAC*)

A Buchon 'undressed', showing its Rolls-Royce Merlin engine, which, with similar irony, also powered the CASA2.111 'He 111s' used in the film. (*PAC*)

G-AWHA low over Duxford and with both engines now running. (*PAC*)

Five Spitfires and a Hurricane at Hawkinge. Spitfire CD-M is actually MH434, the most famous movie Spitfire of all, having since appeared in so many films, and still airworthy at Duxford, operated by the Old Flying Machine Company. (*PAC*)

In what today would be condemned as wanton vandalism, Duxford's single-bay hangar is blown up and destroyed during the film's airfield bombing scene. (*PAC*)

Film Me 109 C4K-152 (G-AWHR) in storage after filming at Wilson Edwards' Big Spring facility. (*PAC*)

'Front of house' film still of the French airfield attack. (*PAC*)

'Achtung! Schpitfeur!' (*John Rush Collection* [*hereafter acknowledged JRC*])

A red-nosed 'Me 109' at Duxford. (*GBC*)

'Red 9' taxiing out at Duxford. (*GBC*)

"We either stand down or blow up. Which do you want?"
Michael Caine

Surprisingly accidents during filming were few and far between. One of the Messerschmitts, C4K-61 (G-AWHF), ground-looped on landing after a filming flight on 21 May and would not take part in any further filming. Wilson 'Connie' Edwards, one of the American Confederate Air Force pilots working on the film, belly landed one of the two-seat Spitfires IXs, MJ772 (G-AVAV), at Little Staughton on 9th July after suffering engine failure during one of the filming sorties.

One of the taxying Spitfires collided with a camera crew at Duxford, thankfully without any major injuries to the crew or damage to the aircraft, during a take-off scene. Taxier Mk XVI TE384 was tipped on its nose at North Weald by accident but left as field dressing for a period. Shortly after, possibly the next day, Robert Shaw stuck taxier Mk XVI SM411 on its nose by over enthusiastic use of the brakes whilst being towed by ropes out of frame.

One of the film's 'Few' was Squadron Leader Mike Vickers. Mike at that time was a QFI at RAF Valley and was coming to the end of his posting at the base. After having served in the Fleet Air Arm during the war, aboard HMS *Formidable* in the Pacific, Mike transferred to the RAF in 1949 and had flown many hours in piston-engined aircraft. He was just what the film's flying unit was looking for. After being selected, the then 44-year-old Mike reported to Duxford on 24 April 1968, to meet Wing Commander George Elliot, who was the 'flying boss' for the RAF side of the operation.

"I was the first of those selected to arrive", remembered Mike Vickers in 1999, "so George Elliot made me his number two. That afternoon, George, who was the only really operational Spitfire pilot amongst us, checked me out on one of the film's two-seat Spitfires. I was subsequently given the task of checking out the rest of the pilots from the RAF as they arrived. We were initially based at RAF Debden, which was then the RAF Police Dog Training School, and we carried out most of the 'work up' flying, plus some of the early filming from there.

"As the various Spitfires and Hurricanes were made ready at Henlow they needed air testing and flying over to Debden. On one occasion I went over to Henlow to test and hopefully bring back Spitfire IIa P7350,

Spitfire AR213. (*GBC*)

which had actually flown in the real Battle of Britain. When I got the aircraft airborne, I noticed that the radiator temperature was rising rapidly, so I quickly had to throttle back and return to the airfield."

It transpired that Mike's problem with the Spitfire was caused by a blocked radiator, a common occurrence with some of the film's aircraft, which had been sat around in museums for some considerable time. After the radiator had been flushed out a couple of times the fighter was deemed to be ready for collection. This was plainly not the case, as Mike recalled:

"On the day I collected the Spitfire, it happened again. I arrived overhead Debden only to find the radiator temperature soaring over the limit. On that occasion I had to shut the engine down and carry out a glide approach and landing. As the aerial shooting gathered momentum, we operated out of Debden, Duxford, Hawkinge and North Weald. On the odd occasions we also used Netheravon, Lympne and Sywell.

As more aircraft arrived from Henlow we were able to film larger formations, but this sometimes got a little complicated. The flying unit was under the direction of David Bracknell, and each evening we would have a conference when the next day's scenes would be explained. We would decide what was possible from the flying point of view and work out the number of aircraft needed, depending on what we had serviceable at the time.

"If the Messerschmitts or Heinkels were needed, then Santa Cruz would organise that side of the operation. Difficulties would often arise when the Spanish pilots were required to take part in scenes together with the Hurricanes and Spitfires. Only one of the Spanish team understood sufficient English to translate what was required to the rest of the Spanish pilots. Sometimes he got it right and sometimes he didn't, which we generally did not find out until we had got airborne. If the Spanish had taken off first, an initial problem then arose because they would often get lost and stray into controlled airspace, start shouting at each other and block up the radio frequency.

"It was very difficult to restore any semblance of order, but eventually, usually by courtesy of Midlands Radar, we would get the Spanish contingent to re-join and take up their positions for filming. But this was not the end of the problems, as when the director called 'action' we would discover that another misunderstanding had arisen in the translation and the Spaniards would fly off in the wrong direction! Unfortunately, this pantomime happened more than once."

Alarmstart! (GBC)

Battle of Britain: The Movie

> "We were up Sir, trying to knock out the enemy en masse."
> *Patrick Wymark*

During the time the film unit was operating at Duxford, it was visited by the world's press on more than one occasion, and often accompanying the media were former wartime fighter aces from both sides of the conflict. On 26 May Lord Dowding, who many feel was the architect of Britain's victory in 1940, visited the airfield, having previously been to Pinewood Studios for a few days to watch Sir Laurence Olivier taking his part for the cameras.

Vivian Bellamy was present at Duxford on the day of Dowding's visit. "It had been arranged that during a break in filming some of the Spitfires

CK4-127 (G-AWHO) as 'White 3', which also masqueraded as Hurricane 'MI-D'. (*GBC*)

would be flown for Dowding and the press people", remembered Vivian. "Not wanting to be outdone, after the Spitfires had landed, Pedro Santa Cruz and the rest of the Spanish pilots took up all the Messerschmitts and proceeded to carry out a formation roll at 800 feet. It was very impressive to watch."

As with any aerial war film there would be a requirement for pilots and crews to be seen bailing out of their stricken aircraft and parachuting safely to the ground. Several of these would be seen to 'roman candle' (parachute failing to open) as did happen all too often during the war, on both sides of the conflict. For these shots one of the film company's two-seat Spitfires was used, with a dummy strapped to the wing or fitted inside the front cockpit. Dummies were also dropped from the unit's Alouette helicopter. At a given moment the dummy would be released and fall to the ground in camera-shot. It was while the unit was operating out of Duxford that the majority of the film's parachuting scenes were shot. For the successful parachuting descents, a team of stuntmen were employed to carry out this demanding task.

One of these was Derek Baker, a former member of the Parachute Regiment, who has since spent a considerable time in the film industry acting as a stuntman, plus stand-in for such well known stars as Michael Caine, Lewis Collins, Sean Connery and Charlton Heston. Derek acted as the jumpmaster during the filming of *Where Eagles Dare* and has fond memories of flying through the Swiss Alps in a Junkers Ju 52. He also participated in the productions of *The Eagle Has Landed*, *Batman* and the James Bond films *On Her Majesty's Secret Service*, *Octopussy*, *A View to a Kill* and *The Living Daylights*.

"I was interviewed and taken on by Sydney Streeter, the film's Production Supervisor", said Derek in a 1997 interview with the author. "My main involvement was at Duxford, during August and September 1968. We had a group of people who were designated as the jump team working in conjunction with Jeff Hawke in the camera ship. It was our job to co-ordinate the various jumps to comply with what Guy Hamilton wanted on any particular day. The weather had to be just right of course, too low cloud and it was not worth jumping in the first place, and if the wind was too strong, we would be blown away from the drop zone. We fitted up a sort of children's slide in the lower gun gondola in the two Heinkel bombers, so that we could slide straight out in a safe exit from the aircraft. We all had to wear the appropriate costumes, depending on whether we were supposed to be portraying the British or Germans, and these costumes had to be modified for us to use.

"We were using the wartime round canopy, but we also had reserve parachutes in case the round ones didn't deploy properly. The seat-type parachute pack, where the round canopy was supposed to deploy from, was in actual fact the housing for the reserve system. The main canopy was attached with a belly-band to our chests and in to a cable system up on top of our shoulder. As we exited the aircraft, we pulled the main chute on our chest, which fired out and as soon as it was open, we then released the belly-band. This fell away, so that when we came into camera view there was nothing on our chest and the flapping seat-type parachute pack was still in place with the reserve if we needed it. I suppose we carried out about 25 jumps in all, and the director then picked which ones he wanted to use in the finished film.

"A Dragon Rapide was used on one occasion when the director wanted to film a series of parachute jumps with people in different costumes.

Buchons good to go. (*GBC*)

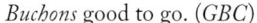

Groundcrews prepare Buckons for a 'mission against England' at El Corpero airfield, Spain. (*GBC*)

We took off from Duxford and dropped on the far side of the airfield. I also did the Polish Hurricane pilot jump, when he lands in the cornfield and the farmers rush up to him with the pitchforks. When you see the long shot of the pilot coming down to the ground, that's me on the end of the parachute. The film then cuts into close-up with the actor taking off the parachute harness. I jumped out of the Alouette helicopter for that shot."

Derek spent seven weeks working on the film and the Hurricane bailout scene was filmed on his 30th birthday. Unbeknown to him, Guy Hamilton knew this and asked Derek do the shot twice. On the second

94 Battle of Britain: The Movie

'take' all the film crew burst into 'Happy Birthday' as Derek floated to the ground in the field!

"Silence, in Polish!"
Barry Foster

The bombing of Duxford Airfield is one of the most impressive scenes in the film, but this sequence alone has been the subject of more debate than any other in the film's history. At the time of filming, no future purpose had been found for Duxford. There was talk of it being converted into an Open Prison after the film unit had left, by which

Buchon pilots. (*GBC*)

token some of the airfield's buildings would be demolished to make way for new ones.

Duxford's Belfast Truss hangars had been in existence since the First World War, but one would bite the dust in the most controversial part of the film company's involvement with the airfield. After much debate between the producers and director as to whether Spitfire Productions had actually got permission to blow up any of the airfield's buildings, it was decided to go ahead with the main airfield attack scene on 21 June.

Mike Vickers remembers this day well: "Paths were marked out with white tape to indicate safe passage between the explosive charges, which had been buried in the grass. The explosions were then triggered off as we were taxying our aircraft along the safe paths. No one had, however, thought of all the smoke, dust and debris which would reduce the visibility to zero. After the explosions started, we could not see the marked lanes at all and therefore the scene became very hairy".

Indeed, it was during this sequence that one of the Spitfires inadvertently taxied into one of the camera crews, thankfully doing little damage.

Earlier in the day, special effects co-ordinators Cliff Richardson and Glenn Robinson prepared the hangar for 'demolition'. They placed inside half a ton of gelignite and three full oil bowsers, all of which were wired up to the main control panel.

As the Spitfires scrambled a series of charges were set off down the airfield to simulate a stick of bombs falling from the marauding Heinkels. When it came to the big hangar explosion, nothing happened! The charges placed inside had failed to detonate. 'Cut', called Guy Hamilton, and all eyes then turned to Richardson and Robinson. With their considerable reputations firmly on the line, they walked into the hangar. This was at great risk to themselves, as the explosive could still ignite! After checking the system, and making good all the fuses and relay switches, they emerged and said that the hangar was ready. By this time the light had started to diminish and the hangar explosion sequence was postponed until the following day.

On 22 June the crew assembled again, and with a great sense of relief on the part of Cliff and Glenn, the hangar went up in a tremendous sheet of flame and smoke. Expertly cut in to the previous day's shooting by the film's editing team, this, on screen, looks like one long continuous 'take'. It was during the bombing of Duxford that a good number of the replica

American Confederate Air Force Colonel Wilson 'Connie' Edwards was amongst civilian pilots flying warbirds during filming. (*GBC*)

aircraft met their end. Some were simply blown to bits where they stood, others had a more complex role to play. When one sees a Spitfire crash into a fuel bowser, it was a carefully wired replica, which was guided to follow a particular path and then hit the tanker. On impact the explosives crew detonated the charge to blow up the fuel tanker. The replica was taxied by Ken King and Les Steele, who were in charge of the replica aircraft effects. Pulling the Spitfire along on a pair of wires it was guided towards the bowser and the rest is history. Sadly, in the finished film, the vehicle explodes a split second before the Spitfire hits it, and there is the sound of screeching tyres, which considering that the Spitfire is taxying on grass, was a bit of an oversight on somebody's part in the sound department!

With the typically British summer disrupting the aerial scenes, time was running out for Hamilton to capture the required flying footage. In an effort to get some better weather and with it the chance to finish off the dogfight sequences, it was decided to take some of the aircraft down to the south of France, where it was hoped that the sun would be out and the skies would be blue.

Mike Vickers was one of the pilots to go on this 'jaunt': "We took nine Spitfires (G-AIST, ASJV, ASSD, AVDJ, AWGB, AWIJ, AB910, PM631 and PS853), three Messerschmitts (G-AWHC, AWHH and AWHT) and the Mitchell to Montpellier. On August 10th we took off from Duxford and cleared customs at Cambridge Airport. Flying in

A very lucky man: *Buchon* pilot. (*GBC*)

Buchons undergoing maintenance – six taxiing examples were made available for filming which were fitted with three-bladed propellers, unlike the four of this airworthy pair. *(GBC)*

easy stages via Le Touquet, Dinard for a night stop, Bordeaux, where we stopped for refuelling, and then onto Montpellier. Our arrival made the television, radio and newspapers and there was quite a crowd to greet us. We spent nine happy and gastronomic days filming in the Mediterranean sunshine, and drinking good French wine.

"However, the Camargue or the Etang du Thau did not bear much resemblance to the south-east of England, so I think that some of the footage we shot there was wasted and was never used in the film. It was with some reluctance that we retraced our steps to Cambridge, stopping this time at Bordeaux, refuelling at Nantes and Le Touquet, before arriving back at Duxford on the evening of August 22nd. After a short time renewing our acquaintances with our families, we were back struggling with the British weather."

At this stage the film was reportedly costing somewhere in the region of £20,000 per day, the original ten to twelve-week schedule for the filming of the aerial sequences had gone 'out of the window' and there were still scenes to be completed. By now the Spanish Air Force pilots were having to return home as their 'leave of absence' was coming to an end. It was another crisis point for *Battle of Britain*.

"Because the Spaniards were leaving, some of us were converted onto the Messerschmitts", remembered Mike Vickers. "At that time I also got involved in some of the camerawork myself. There were a couple of scenes which required shooting from inside the cockpit of a Spitfire, one was of Simon, a new pilot with little experience, becoming disorientated and getting lost in the sky, before being shot down by a Messerschmitt."

> "If we're right, they'll give up. If we're wrong,
> they'll be in London in a week."
> *Laurence Olivier*

A *Buchon* rather the worse for wear. (*GBC*)

By the end of September, the contract which allowed Spitfire Productions to operate out of Duxford was coming to an end, some of the RAF pilots were having to return to their parent units, leaving just a handful of service and civilian personnel on the flying unit. Work at Duxford was wrapped up and the unit moved to Bovingdon in an attempt to put the final sequences 'in the can'. It was while operating out of Bovingdon that special clearance had to be obtained for the two Heinkels to fly up the River Thames estuary for the blitz scenes in the film. The last location filming took place at was Netheravon, when Mike Vickers and some of the remaining pilots carried out some more dummy pilot parachute drops for the cameras.

"On October 22nd, almost six months to the day of my arrival at Duxford, the aerial unit ceased to operate", recalls Mike. "I had personally flown 110 hours in the Spitfires, 20 on the Messerschmitts and five on the Hurricanes. Those weeks had turned out to be one of the most interesting and exciting periods of my flying career." (Mike Vickers returned to his normal duties and finally retired from the RAF in 1978. He subsequently joined Oxford Air Training School at Kidlington Airport and spent several years training commercial pilots and instructors. He retired in 1992, after 50 years of flying, with 17,500 hours and 120 different types in his logbook.)

Some 110 hours of pure flying scenes had been shot, which had to be edited down to the 40 minutes required for the finished film. The aircraft employed in the production had, in total, clocked up some 5,000 flying hours re-creating Britain's Finest Hour. It had, in anybody's book, been an epic effort.

Aircraft leased from their civilian owners, and those borrowed on occasion from the Battle of Britain Flight quickly returned to their rightful homes, while the various MoD aircraft were put back to their original configurations at Henlow, from whence they were re-allocated to RAF stations around the UK. Those aircraft purchased by Hamish Mahaddie, on behalf of Spitfire Productions were offered for immediate disposal. A late 1968 document contained those aircraft 'up for grabs', with a set of prices, which today would seem too good to be true. Heinkel IIIs G-AWHA and G-AWHB, both in flying condition, were offered for £7,000 and £6,000 respectively. Two Messerschmitt 109s, which had been mocked up with dummy radiator scoops for a possible role in the

Spitfires undergoing maintenance. (*GBC*)

film *Patton*, were priced at £7,500 each or £14,000 for the pair. Five of the six taxying Messerschmitts, which were still located in Spain, could be acquired for £2,000 each, or £8,500 for all five. The two Spitfire Tr.9s, which had valid certificates of airworthiness, commanded a higher price of £12,000 each, while one of the 'spare' Spitfires, a Griffon-engined Mk.XIV, was available for £4,750. The Canadian-built Hurricane G-AWLW was in the Spitfire Tr.9 price league and was for sale at £12,000. Also listed for sale at the same time was Mahaddie's DH Mosquito B/TT.35 G-ASKB, star of *633 Squadron* and *Mosquito Squadron*. This was on offer for the princely sum of £9,000!

And so, the world's 35th largest air force was dispersed. With upwards of 100 vintage aircraft under their command, producers Saltzman and Fisz had achieved what they set out to do. They had created a lasting celluloid tribute to 'The Few'.

It was now the turn of the backroom boys at Pinewood Studios to put the story together, editing the mass of film footage, creating the special effects, and finally matching the soundtrack music to the action on the screen.

Reel 10

Identifying the Royal Air Force

It is an easy task these days to identify vintage aircraft when they appear at airshows, for even if they are wearing representative markings, more often than not the airframe carries its original serial. During the filming of *Battle*, with all the aircraft wearing 'uniform' colours and

WAAF 'Corporal Seymour' (Pat Heywood) and Susannah York (Section Officer Maggie Harvey) prepare for a scene at Duxford. (*GBC*)

Michael Caine (Squadron Leader Canfield) and Christopher Plummer (Squadron Leader Harvey) await their next scene; Plummer died in 2021. (*GBC*)

markings, it was much more difficult to work out which aircraft was which. The airworthy Spitfires, Hurricanes and Messerschmitts reportedly had their true identities painted on the inside of the wheel wells and on the flaps in the case of the Messerschmitts, which was all very well if you were one of the fortunate ones who were able to inspect the 'stars' at close quarters. But for today's keen aviation film fans, some of whom were not even born when the film was being made, the problem of identifying the individual 'performers' has proved to be somewhat problematical.

This guide is not intended to be infallible, but will certainly help to identify the individual airframes. This system really only works for the flyable Spitfires and Hurricanes used. As for the Messerschmitts and

Heinkels, these aircraft were virtually identical and carried no major distinguishing features, save that the taxying Messerschmitts, used only in Spain, were fitted with three blade propellers and the flyable airframes, which came to the UK, were fitted with four blade units.

Through a system of noting the number of propeller blades, exhaust stacks, wheel apertures, radiators, paint stains etc, and much study of photographic evidence, it is possible to pin down the individual airworthy Spitfires and Hurricanes which were used in the filming. It is possible to identify the taxying and static Spitfires, but it has to be said, it is a little more problematic!

Supermarine Spitfires (Airworthy)

Spitfire IA AR213	4 blade prop, 6 tubular exhaust stubs, small aperture Perspex window in front of and below windscreen, internal armour-plated windscreen, 5 aperture wheels.
Spitfire IIA P7350	3 blade broad chord root Dowty prop, 3 fishtail exhaust stubs, external armour-plated windscreen, 5 aperture wheels.
Spitfire VB AB910	4 blade prop, 6 tubular exhaust stubs, internal armour-plated windscreen, 4 aperture wheels.
Spitfire VC AR501	3 blade narrow chord DH prop, 6 fishtail exhaust stubs, internal armour-plated windscreen, 5 aperture wheels.
Spitfire IX MH415	4 blade prop, initially 6 fishtail exhaust stubs but later 6 tubular exhaust stubs, 4 aperture wheels, strobe lights in gun ports.
Spitfire IX MH434	4 blade prop, 6 tubular exhaust stubs, 4 aperture wheels, small dipole aerial under rear fuselage.
Spitfire IX MK297	4 blade prop, 6 fishtail exhaust stubs, 4 aperture wheels.
Spitfire Tr IX MJ772	4 blade prop, 6 fishtail exhaust stubs, 4 aperture wheels.
Spitfire Tr IX TE308	4 blade prop, 6 tubular exhaust stubs, 3 aperture wheels, fitted with Buchon prop and spinner at one stage of filming.

Spitfire XIV RM689   Griffon engine, 5 blade prop, rear fuselage whip radio aerial, retractable tailwheel permanently locked down, standard framed windscreen.

Spitfire PR XIX PM631   Griffon engine, 5 blade prop, rear fuselage whip radio aerial, 3 aperture wheels, retractable tailwheel, one-piece non-framed windscreen.

Spitfire PR XIX PS853   Griffon engine, 5 blade prop, rear fuselage whip radio aerial, 3 aperture wheels, cabin air pressurisation intake on port engine cowling, retractable tailwheel, one-piece non-framed windscreen.

A suitable system for identifying the taxying and static Spitfires used in the film has been much more difficult to pin down. Suffice to say that

Group Captain Townsend receives a briefing on a *Buchon* from Commandante Pedro Santa Cruz at Tablada, 1968. (*GBC*)

Group Captain Bader with (from left) Robert Shaw ('Squadron Leader "Skipper"'), Christopher Plummer ('Squadron Leader Harvey') and Group Captain Townsend at Duxford, 1968. (*GBC*)

the majority of the airframes were given the *Mark Addie* treatment to portray a 'uniform' effect on screen. An easy to distinguish feature of the *Mark Addie*'s is that none of the airframes have trim tabs fitted to the rudders, due to these components all being removed and modified during the aircraft's conversion process.

The following selection of 'de-codes' gives a guide for aircraft identification purposes. (Note: as of 2021 with substantially more images accumulated, the taxying and static Spitfires can all now be confidently identified, principally by studying, comparing and 'finger printing' the unique distress staining, paint chips and accumulated ageing of the livery).

Supermarine Spitfires (Taxying & Static)

Note Mk Vs have a short Merlin engine, whereas Mk IXs and XVIs have a long a Merlin.

Spitfire Vb BL614	4 blade prop, 3 fishtail exhaust stubs, 3 aperture wheels, metal repair plate on sliding cockpit canopy.
Spitfire Vb EP120	4 blade prop, 6 tubular exhaust stubs, internal armour-plated windscreen, 4 aperture wheels, no wingtip navigation lights.
Spitfire IX MK356	4 blade prop, 6 fishtail exhaust stubs, 4 aperture wheels, metal repair patch on rear cockpit Perspex.
Spitfire XVIe RW382	4 blade prop, 6 tubular exhaust stacks, 3 aperture wheels, Czech roundel by windscreen for a period.
Spitfire XVIe SL574	4 blade prop, 3 fishtail exhaust stubs, 3 aperture wheels.
Spitfire XVIe SM411	3 blade DH prop, 6 tubular exhaust stubs, no wingtip navigation lights.
Spitfire XVIe TB382	3 blade Dowty prop, 6 tubular exhaust stubs, no wingtip navigation lights.
Spitfire XVIe TE311	4 blade prop, 6 tubular exhaust stacks, one distorted on port side, 3 aperture wheels.
Spitfire XVIe TE356	4 blade prop, 6 tubular exhaust stacks, 3 aperture wheels.
Spitfire XVIe TE384	4 blade prop, 6 tubular exhaust stacks, 3 aperture wheels.
Spitfire XVIe TE476	3 blade Dowty prop, 6 tubular exhaust stacks, 4 aperture wheel port, 5 aperture wheel starboard.
Spitfire PR.XIX PM651	Griffon engine, 5 blade prop, rear fuselage whip radio aerial, 3 aperture wheels, retractable tailwheel, one-piece non-framed windscreen. Top engine cowl removed for maintenance shots.

Spitfire PR.XIX PS915	Griffon engine, 5 blade prop, rear fuselage whip radio aerial, 3 aperture wheels, retractable tailwheel, one-piece non-framed windscreen. Top engine cowl removed for maintenance shots.
Spitfire F.21 LA198	5 blade prop, 3 aperture wheels, non-elliptical wings, flush navigation lights on wingtips, additional undercarriage doors.

Hawker Hurricanes (Airworthy)

Hurricane IIC LF363	6 exhaust stubs, circular rear-view mirror, straight radio aerial, 'knuckle-style' tailwheel oleo leg.
Hurricane IIC PZ865	6 exhaust stubs, rectangular rear-view mirror, rearwards leaning radio aerial, 'knuckle-style' tailwheel oleo leg.
Hurricane XII G-AWLW	flat Canadian-style prop spinner, 3 tubular exhaust stubs, single oleo strut tailwheel.

Hawker Hurricanes (Taxying)

Hurricane I P2617	3 tubular exhaust stubs, no rear-view mirror, 'knuckle-style' tailwheel oleo leg. (So far as can be ascertained, P2617 was not actually used in the film, although it did go to Henlow.)
Sea Hurricane I Z7015	3 tubular exhaust stubs, broad chord three-blade propeller, single oleo strut tailwheel.

Reel 11

Music Maketh the Movie

The music for the soundtrack of *Battle of Britain*, and how it came to be written and recorded, was not itself without controversy. It had originally been contracted out to the famous composer Sir William Walton to compose and record, but Walton, who had previously scored such films as *Henry V*, *The First of the Few*, *Went The Day Well* and *The Foreman Went To France*, only wrote around 20 minutes of music for *Battle of Britain*. When the heads of United Artists heard the music, they

A still from the French airfield attack scene, Duxford 1968. (*GBC*)

A replica 'Mark Addie' Spitfire arriving at Duxford. (*GBC*)

rejected it. One of the reasons is thought to be that there was not enough music to fill a long-playing (LP) soundtrack record!

This rejection took place around a month before the film was due to be premiered and the rush was then on to find another suitable composer.

The producers duly contacted one of the best-known film music composers in the UK, Ron Goodwin. Goodwin's previous film scores had included some of the most popular British box office hits of all time (including a fair number of aviation films): *633 Squadron*, *Where Eagles Dare*, *Operation Crossbow*, *Those Magnificent Men in their Flying Machines*, as well as *Monte Carlo or Bust*, *The Trap* and the Miss Marple films, among many others.

In a 1995 interview with the author, Ron Goodwin recalled the writing of *Battle of Britain*'s music score: "Film producer Ben Fisz, whom I'd never met before, telephoned me one day and asked if I'd go over to his office in Mayfair, London, to see him. So I went along, and he said to me 'We're making this film *Battle of Britain* and I'd like you to write the music. There is just one problem. We've already had a score written by Sir William Walton which we don't want to use.'

"I wasn't too happy about that, because I didn't want to get into a public competition with somebody as well-known as Walton, because I knew who would lose!"

Fisz assured Goodwin that only his score would be used and that nobody would even know that there had been any music composed for *Battle of Britain* by William Walton. Ron accepted the commission, but purposely did not listen to any of the music composed by Walton, as he wanted to create his own score for the film. By this time, it was only three weeks before the film's fixed premiere date in London (15 September 1969), so Ron had to work quickly if a suitable score was to be ready in time.

So desperate were the producers that Fisz told Goodwin that he could name his own fee if he could deliver the music in time.

"I named a figure, which was quite a good one for that time, and set to work", remembers Ron, "and then the trouble started. About a week before the studio recording date Harry Saltzman called me and said 'Can you come and see me in my office, it's very urgent'. I reminded him that time was of the essence if I was going to finish all of the music that the

Hurricane replica. (*GBC*)

Director Guy Hamilton demonstrates how he wants it done. (*GBC*)

producers wanted for the film, but Saltzman insisted that I go and see him in London. When I got to Saltzman's office he told me that Sir Laurence Olivier was very upset that Walton's music was not going to be used, and unless some of Walton's score is retained in the film he (Olivier) is going to have his name taken off the film."

For a major actor like Olivier to have his name removed from the movie's credits would have been the kiss of death to a production like *Battle of Britain*. The adverse publicity it would have incurred could have had drastic effects on the film's release, and in turn its overall box office viability. Something obviously had to be done, and done quickly!

Even though he was originally promised that it would be his score and his score alone that was heard in the film, Ron was then asked if he would agree to some of Walton's music being inserted into the soundtrack of the production. This delicate matter was then put into the hands of Ron's lawyer, Stanley Rubenstein who advised Saltzman and Fisz that they had gone back on their promise that only Goodwin's music would be used.

"However, the producers were very crafty", remembers Ron, "because they suggested that possibly Walton's music for the 'Battle in the Air' sequence towards the end of the film could be slotted in without any problems. 'Why don't we listen to your music for that section of the film and then listen to Walton's and decide which one we like the best,' Saltzman said to me. It was all a bit of a joke really because it was obvious which one they were going to pick."

Inevitably Walton's music for the 'Battle in the Air' sequence was decided upon, but as Ron remembers: "My lawyer and I went to the press show of the film on September 15th, before the official public premiere later that day, and that was the first that we knew that the producers had used Walton's music for the aforementioned sequence. To make matters worse, after the press show, someone at United Artists dubbed in several bars of William Walton's end theme as the closing credits were rolling up the screen, then it faded out and my theme was faded in. It sounded like a really serious dubbing error. I've subsequently seen it on television with this 'altered' ending, and I've also seen another version with my full end title music intact. So, at some stage in the proceedings there were two different prints of the film floating around. I presume this was done so that the producers could say that both pieces of music were used!"

Myles Hoyle ('Peter') taking direction from Guy Hamilton. (*GBC*)

Indeed, the first time that *Battle of Britain* was shown on British television (BBC One in September 1974, five years from the film's original cinema release) it was a print with the Walton/Goodwin end title theme. This version of the film has never been released on video. All video/DVD copies have the complete Goodwin end title theme intact. On 23 January 1999, Channel Four television broadcast a copy of *Battle of Britain* which had the William Walton end title music intact with none of Goodwin's familiar theme included at all, thus making a third variation of extant prints of the film.

"The sad part of the whole affair", says Ron, "is that United Artists never even told Sir William Walton that his music had been dropped from the film! The first he knew of the problem was when a film critic rang Walton to ask him why his music was not used in the film. Then the press got hold of the story and there were articles in the newspapers asking why Sir William Walton OM had his score replaced by one Ron Goodwin, who has yet to receive his Order of Merit? It was all spiteful stuff, which one could have done without, and I suddenly became 'the villain of the piece' overnight."

Ron Goodwin's score for *Battle of Britain* contains one of the best pieces of martial music ever recorded for the big screen. *Luftwaffe March* is heard over the titles as General Milch inspects the lines of Heinkel bombers and their crews on the film's French airfields. Indeed, it has

'Lights! Camera! Action!' (*GBC*)

been said by many that *Luftwaffe March* is the 'star' piece of music in the film!

"Some people questioned where my loyalties lay when they heard Luftwaffe March, but that's probably because it is the first music heard in the film," says Ron, "and that it's such a dramatic and dominant piece. The producers told me that the Germans were victorious at the beginning of the film and the British were victorious at the end, therefore this should be reflected in the accompanying music. I based the Luftwaffe March on all the German marches I'd ever heard; because they've all got that heavy, relentless beat to them. In fact, the Luftwaffe March took me most of the three weeks to compose and get right. It was really panic stations to get the whole score completed. I had to work through the night on several occasions in order to finish the music and get it orchestrated in time for the recording sessions."

This 'panic situation' certainly does not seem apparent when one listens to Goodwin's music for *Battle of Britain*, for it ably conveys the might of the Luftwaffe, whilst the RAF portions of the score are truly patriotic and gained cheers from the cinema audiences when the RAF was getting the upper hand halfway through the film!

Goodwin's score for the film was released on the United Artists long playing record *Battle of Britain* (UAS 29019 in the UK, MCA-25008 in the USA) and eight-track tape cartridge (8XU 29019) to coincide with the film's 1969 premiere and featured 19 tracks:

Side One

1: *Battle of Britain* Theme, 2: Luftwaffe March; 3: The Lull Before the Storm; 4: Work and Play; 5: Death and Destruction; 6: Briefing the Luftwaffe; 7: Prelude to Battle; 8: Victory Assured; 9: Defeat.

Side Two

1: Hitler's Headquarters; 2: Return to Base; 3: Threat; 4: Civilian Tragedy; 5: Offensive Build-up; 6: Attack; 7: Personal Tragedy; 8: Battle in the Air (Composed by Sir William Walton OM and conducted by Malcolm Arnold); 9: Absent Friends; 10: *Battle of Britain* Theme – End Title.

'Me 109s' attack an 'RAF airfield in France'. (*GBC*)

After being deleted for many years, the soundtrack was digitally remastered and released in 1990 on Compact Disc (CD) by EMI in the UK (CDP 79 4865 2). This re-release coincided with the 50th anniversary of the 1940 Battle of Britain, but after around 12 months in the record shops this CD was deleted from the catalogue.

Up to 1999, Sir William Walton's full score for the film had never been issued on record or compact disc. The publishers, Oxford University Press (OUP) were due to release the music, indeed some of it had been programmed for inclusion in the BBC's Henry Wood Promenade Concert in 1969, as part of the film's publicity campaign, but it was withdrawn at the last minute and the music subsequently disappeared.

Later, the Rt Hon Edward Heath (when he was the UK's Prime Minister) was able to obtain the score from OUP's vaults, and with the permission of Saltzman and Fisz, who owned the rights to the music, presented a copy of it to Sir William Walton, during a private dinner party at No.10 Downing Street in 1972 to celebrate the composer's 70th birthday.

In the same year (1990) that Ron Goodwin's music for *Battle of Britain* was re-released on Compact Disc, portions of the Walton score surfaced on a CD marketed by Chandos in the UK, 'Sir William Walton's Film Music Vol 2' (CHAN 8870). Sir Neville Marriner conducting The Academy of St Martin in the Fields recorded three individual pieces. Scherzo – Gay Berlin; Spitfire Music and Battle in the Air; March Introduction, March and Siegfried Music. The latter two movements formed a concert suite arranged by Colin Matthews and were performed in public during the mid-1980s by renowned composer and conductor Carl Davis.

Goodwin's own *Battle of Britain* Suite, a compilation of his different themes from the film, has been a popular inclusion in many of Ron's concerts throughout the world. It was finally recorded at a live concert at London's Royal Festival Hall in 1996 and released on a CD in 1998 entitled 'Screen Extravaganza' (Music Collection International, MPMCD2 004).

In May 1999 a major breakthrough took place, when the American-based company Rykodisc released a CD (RCD 10747) which included all of Goodwin's score, plus the entire selection of music composed for the film by Sir William Walton. That Walton's music should resurface after nearly 30 years was nothing short of a miracle. When the original 1969 recording sessions took place at the Anvil Studios at Denham, the then recording engineer Eric Tomlinson had the incredible foresight to keep hold of three 'master back-up' reels of tape.

He 111 and bombload. (*GBC*)

Taking them home, he stored them in his garage and over the years forgot all about them. In the 1990s the tapes were re-discovered having gathered much dust and mould over two decades. Many hours of painstaking work went into the remastering of Walton's music, until finally it was ready for release. On listening to Sir William's offering, it includes many of the trademarks of a Walton score. Indeed, his *Battle of Britain* March has audible overtones of one of his earlier compositions, 'Orb and Sceptre'.

Assisting Walton with the orchestration was his friend and fellow composer, Malcolm Arnold, who had been heavily involved in the scoring of many films. Arnold conducted the recording sessions of Walton's score, and reportedly also assisted in the composing of certain passages.

Whatever the controversy and internal politics surrounding the final musical choice used in the film, Ron Goodwin's music for Battle of Britain has stood the test of time and has gone down in history as one of the most charismatic and descriptive scores ever composed for an aviation film!

Enthusiast Paul Robinson adds the following: "The battle over the film score has a well-documented history. The current Blu Ray release features only the Goodwin score with Walton's 'Battle in the Air'. However, if the Italian language track option is selected, several of William Walton's original cues are heard. To confuse matters further, their place on the soundtrack differs from their place on the 'restored' Walton soundtrack available as an option on the 'Special Edition' DVD.

"The first instance occurs following the bombing of the airfield represented by Duxford. As Maggie walks solemnly over to the hastily covered bodies of the dead WAAFs laid on the grass by the bombed slit trench, the music changes abruptly from Goodwin's cue to Walton's. Another example of the music substitution comes as Harvey calls out 'Home and Tea, for once you deserve it,' just before the solo Spitfire does a victory roll over the airfield at Hawkinge.

"When film prints are sent to non-English speaking countries, they begin with what was known as an M and E track, that is music and effects only. Actors speaking that country's native language then have their scripted translation of the original dialogue added to the M and E track before the final sound mix is created. In the case of the Italian track, it is possible that the M and E track supplied used an earlier sound

Christopher Plummer and Guy Hamilton working on the French airfield scene whilst codes are applied to the aircraft. (*GBC*)

mix completed before Ron Goodwin's score was chosen. Though why examples of both scores appear to have been used for this particular sound mix remains a mystery.

"Original cinema prints released in Germany also differed. In place of Goodwin's familiar *Luftwaffe March* heard during the opening title's inspection sequence, and again during the scene showing Goering's arrival by train, two traditional German marches, Preussens Gloria and the Badenweiler Marsch, were used instead. These both featured on the German soundtrack LP while some of Ron Goodwin's cues did not.

"Anyone familiar with the original film music soundtrack versions released over the years, will have noticed a track entitled *Absent Friends*.

This cue by Ron Goodwin was not used in the final cinema release, however played against the film from the scene showing Falke and his colleagues seated around the dining table bedecked with several laurel wreaths, up to the shot of the fire engine passing the entrance to the tube station, the music fits perfectly. Given the cues title, this is probably where it's originally intended placement in the film was.

"Ron Goodwin's original cue, written for the decisive 15th September 1940 battle, which was not used rather than Walton's 'Battle in the Air,' has yet to be released and remains unheard and unknown to this day. Hopefully one day the opportunity will arrive when fans of the film will

Producer Ben Fisz and Director Guy Hamilton – the two men who made *Battle of Britain* happen. (*GBC*)

be able to watch the final battle with either composer's interpretation of that climatic sequence."

Ron Goodwin

Ron Goodwin was born in Plymouth on 17 February 1925. A highly successful film music composer and conductor, Ron was without doubt one of the UK entertainment industry's most versatile and complete musical talents. After leaving school he began working in an insurance agency and playing trumpet in a band in his spare time, he was advised by his then employer to go and get a job in the music industry. After spending a period in the copying department of music publishers Campbell Connelly and Co, he started to provide arrangements for some of the leading recording artists of the 1950s, Jimmy Young and Petula Clark, to name just two. Ron also arranged the orchestral accompaniment for the very popular Peter Sellers comedy records, *Goodness Gracious Me* and *Balham – Gateway to the South* etc.

His first score for the silver screen was for the 1958 film *Whirlpool*, going on to compose the music for over 60 feature films, including some of the biggest British box office successes ever. The series of four Miss Marple films (with Margaret Rutherford), *633 Squadron* (the first British-made war film in Panavision and colour), *Those Magnificent Men in their Flying Machines* and the sequel *Monte Carlo or Bust* (or as it was called in America, *Those Daring Young Men in their Jaunty Jalopies*), *Frenzy*, *The Trap*, *Day of the Triffids*, *Lancelot and Guinevere*, *Force Ten from Navarone*, *Operation Crossbow*, *The Early Bird* (with Norman Wisdom), *That Rivera Touch* (with Morecambe and Wise), *Submarine XI*, *Where Eagles Dare*, and many others.

In 1993 Ron Goodwin was made a Fellow of the City of Leeds College of Music, and in 1994 was presented with an Ivor Novello Award for Life Achievement in Music. A true 'gentleman' of the music business, Ron celebrated his 75th birthday in a special concert of his film music with the Bournemouth Symphony Orchestra at the Winter Gardens Theatre, Bournemouth, on 12 February 2000. He died in 2003.

Sir William Walton

Born in 1902, William Walton was perhaps best known for his scores for *Henry V* (1944), *Hamlet* (1948) and *Richard III* (1956), all of which

Music Maketh the Movie

Producer Ben Fisz – himself a former wartime fighter pilot – with Robert Shaw ('Squadron Leader "Skipper"'). (*GBC*)

starred Laurence Olivier, hence their great friendship. Walton was also instrumental in the composition of music for some of the best known and effective films to emanate from the British film industry during the Second World War, *The Foreman Went To France* (1942), *Went the Day*

Well (1942) and *The First Of The Few* (1942), the latter spawning the all-time classic 'Spitfire Prelude and Fugue'. He composed his first film score in 1935 for *Escape Me Never*, and his last in 1970, *The Three Sisters*. Sir William Walton died in 1983.

Malcolm Arnold
Born on 21 October 1921, at Northampton, England, Arnold studied composition, trumpet and piano at the Royal College of Music, London, in 1938. He joined the Royal Philharmonic Orchestra as a trumpet player in 1940. After serving in the Army between 1944 and 1951, Malcolm Arnold concentrated on composing classical works until his debut as a film music composer in 1952. His films include: *The Sound Barrier* (1952), *Hobson's Choice* (1953), *The Night My Number Came Up* (1955), *A Hill in Korea* (1956), *Blue Murder at St Trinians* (1957), *The Bridge on the River Kwai* (1957), *Dunkirk* (1958), *Inn of the Sixth Happiness* (1958), *The Angry Silence* (1960), *Whistle Down the Wind* (1961), *The Heroes of Telemark* (1965) and *David Copperfield* (1970). Malcolm Arnold died in 2006.

'Take cover!' (*GBC*)

Reel 12

On Release

When *Battle of Britain* was released onto the cinema circuits, 29 years after the real Battle, it was the end of a long, long road for Ben S. Fisz and Harry Saltzman. Through much adversity they had eventually triumphed and created a lasting record of RAF Fighter Command's 'Finest Hour'.

The main premiere took place at the Dominion Theatre, Tottenham Court Road, London, at 8.30pm on Monday 15 September 1969. It was a glittering occasion and was attended by the Right Honourable the Lord Mayor of London, Sir Charles Trinder and the Lady Mayoress, Lady Trinder, who were the guests of honour. Other VIPs included 350 members of the Battle of Britain Fighter Association, not just from the UK, but from as far apart as Canada, Jamaica, Kenya, Saudi Arabia and New Zealand. Chief of the Air Staff, Air Chief Marshal Sir John Grandy, was also present, as was the man who had led 'The Few' to victory in 1940, Lord Hugh Dowding.

Many of the film's stars were also present, as well as some of the original combatants who had acted as technical advisors on the production. To add to the supreme sense of occasion, the Central Band of the RAF, augmented by the Fanfare Trumpeters, played before and after the film.

Simultaneous UK premieres were also held that night in Belfast, Birmingham, Cardiff, Edinburgh, Glasgow, Leeds, Liverpool, Manchester, Newcastle-on-Tyne, Nottingham and Sheffield.

On 20 October a Royal Gala Performance of the film was mounted at the Dominion, and honoured guests for that charity evening, proceeds of which were donated to the RAF Benevolent Fund and the RAF Association, included Her Majesty the Queen, HRH the Prince of Wales, Princess Anne, the Duke and Duchess of Kent, HRH Prince Michael of Kent, HRH Princess Alexandra and the Hon Angus Ogilvy, HRH the Duchess of Gloucester and Chief of the Defence Staff, Marshal of the RAF Sir Charles Elworthy.

The opening credits scene's unforgettable vista of eighteen Spanish-built He 111 bombers. (*GBC*)

All over the world, the film took centre stage, with star-studded premieres in Australia, Austria, Canada, Finland, France, Germany, Greece, Holland, Spain, Switzerland, New Zealand, Norway, and Portugal. France debuted *Battle of Britain* at the Palais de Chaillot, which seated 26,000 people. It was a high-profile charity occasion, sponsored by President Georges Pompidou, which benefited the Free French, the Comité de Libération and the RAF Association. Searchlights picked out aircraft which flew over in a special night-time flypast, and after the showing there was a spectacular firework display at the nearby Eiffel Tower.

Prior to the premieres the film company's publicity machine had been working overtime. All through production there had been regular news updates in the national press and television on the film's progress. Leonard Mosley's book on the making of the film had been serialised in one of the major Sunday newspapers in the weeks leading up to the premiere. Independent Television (ITV) screened an hour-long documentary, *Battle for the Battle of Britain*, produced by Christopher Doll, at 10.45pm on 13 September. This 'behind the scenes' look at the production's trials and tribulations had previously been shown on the American NBC network on 7 September.

'Luftwaffe officers'. (*GBC*)

Battle of Britain: The Movie

On 5 September, Douglas Bader and Ginger Lacey, along with some of the film's cast, were present at the 'switching on' ceremony of the Blackpool Illuminations. In May a special exhibition on the film, including large scale Heinkel and Spitfire replicas, plus a recreation of a Fighter Command 1940 operations room, was opened at Madame Tussauds, London's famous waxworks museum.

While all the pre-publicity was flooding the UK and the rest of the globe, the producers could not do anything to combat the critics and the sometimes less than enthusiastic reviews which followed the film's release. "Not So Hot, This Epic", proclaimed one national newspaper, which went on to say: "Certainly it has good, even magnificent moments, no one could sit through the great aerial ballets without being awed and stirred. Compared with machines, human beings have a raw deal. There is no one the audience can identify with, feel for. The one attempt to introduce a substantial human story – a husband and wife torn by separate war obligations – is trite and unconvincing. The film-makers claim that they wanted documentary authenticity. They may not have adjusted history, but they have thrown no revealing light on it either. Sorry to go on, but when a film is fanfared so loudly as this one, can we be blamed for expecting wonders." Others were not quite so scathing with their critiques: "In 133 minutes, the terror and courage which is

Spitfire MH415. (*GBC*)

called their 'finest hour', Director Guy Hamilton and his team of expert technicians and fliers have strikingly caught the atmosphere of those weeks of destiny. All this, without mock heroics, is brought out in this compelling picture. It is studded with stars and feature players but the real stars are the planes – many of them old crates that fought in the campaign. Considering the wide scope of the subject the producers have done a fine job which will both entertain and, I think, inspire."

In subsequent years, film-listing books have not been so kind. One well known tome describes it as "a plodding attempt to cover an historical event from too many angles and with too many guest stars, all indistinguishable from each other when masked in the cockpit during the repetitive and interminable dogfight sequences". Another regarded it as a "well-meaning but unexciting all-star extravaganza made to mark the 30th anniversary of the 1940 aerial attack on England. A few good cameos, some gripping dogfights and stirring music, but the best thing is the photography. A bit out of its time; the public didn't really want to know, and it lost money."

A third, meanwhile, says: "This stirring if slightly overlong saga of England's WWII defence of its homeland features a staggering star-studded cast, with excellent portrayals down the line, despite the restrictions of their roles. Olivier is in fine form as Sir Hugh Dowding, whose crafty tactics with his limited fighter command induced the Luftwaffe to make fatal errors. Except for Jurgens, however, the German actors are mere caricatures of the Nazi high command, with Rolf Stiefel especially ludicrous as a berserk Hitler. The dogfights between the British and German fighters are spectacular and fascinating."

On the whole, *Battle of Britain* has not enjoyed a good critique over the years. While it may have been made at the wrong time for the cinema audiences to appreciate it, it was made at the right time in terms of the aircraft that appeared in it! Even in this day and age, when the worldwide warbird movement is seemingly in full swing, *Battle of Britain* could not be re-made, although having said that, with CGI, almost anything is possible in the cinema! Even though the film company had gathered together the 35th largest air force in the world, many say that better use could have been made of the aerial hardware. That apart, *Battle of Britain* remains a supreme celluloid example of two air forces fighting it out in the skies above England.

A signed postcard by Robert Shaw. (*Ian Sayer Archive* [*ISA*])

Promotions and Marketing Merchandise
The publicity campaign for *Battle of Britain* was one of the biggest that had been mounted for any motion picture for a long time, and at the time of the film's release a wealth of promotional merchandising was available in many forms. Dinky, the well-known toy and model manufacturer, released a pair of metal Spitfire II and Junkers Ju 87B models. The Spitfire featured a motorised propeller and the Stuka came complete with a cap-firing bomb. Frog models issued a trio of paired aircraft kits, Spitfire & Ju 88, Blenheim & Messerschmitt Bf 109F and Hurricane & Ju 87G Stuka.

Weidenfeld and Nicolson published Leonard Mosley's *The Battle of Britain – The Making of a Film* in hardback for the princely sum of 50 shillings (or £2.50 in today's currency). *The Narrow Margin*, the book by Derek Wood and Derek Dempster, on which the film's screenplay was based, was re-issued in large format softback, with full colour cover photographs from the film. *Pan Books* published a series of eight paperbacks, which included a softback version of Mosley's film book, plus, *Ginger Lacey – Fighter Pilot*, *Squadron Airborne*, *Fighter Pilot*, *The Last Enemy*, *Full Circle*, *Eagle Day* and *Aircraft of the Battle of Britain*, all of which sported new covers featuring the film's logo.

J. Arthur Dixon, the Isle of Wight based postcard manufacturer, was granted a licence to market a series of 32 colour postcards featuring scenes from the film. These could also be mounted in a special album, which contained information about the film and the action depicted on the postcards. The complete set came supplied in a commemorative display box.

BPC Publishing/Purnell produced a series of picture books, colouring books, push-out model books and jigsaws based on the film, while Jackdaw Publications issued a '*Battle of Britain* Folder', which contained reproduction documents, maps and a whole host of 1940-related material. United Artists Records released the original soundtrack recording from the film (see Music Maketh the Movie) on a 33⅓rpm long playing record (UAS 29019), plus a 45rpm single which featured the *Battle of Britain* Theme on the 'A' side and *Luftwaffe March* on the 'B' side (UP 35040), both played by Ron Goodwin.

A. & B.C. Chewing Gum Ltd produced a set of bubblegum cards, issued in packs of seven for 6d. The full set of 66 cards showed scenes from the film in colour, plus facsimile front pages from the *Daily Mirror* newspapers of 1940. Plaistow Press marketed a set of eight 17 x 23in posters showing various aerial scenes from the film, as well as some of the actors. Printed on glossy art card they retailed at 7s 6d each, or 50s for the full set. Wells Soft Drinks produced a series of bottled fizzy drinks with a special 'Bottle' of Britain film label. These were not available for purchase over shop counters, instead being used as a promotional tool for the various cinemas and theatres showing the film throughout the UK.

The film was originally released in the UK on video (VHS PAL) for the first time in 1983, when Warner Home Video (WHV) issued it in large box format (PEV 99292). Since then *Battle of Britain* has been re-issued on a regular basis. As of 2021, editions of the film exist in widescreen on both DVD and Blue-ray and digital download via Amazon prime and alike. The documentary made charting the film's, production titled *Battle for the Battle of Britain* produced by Christopher Doll is also available as a

A signed photograph by Susannah York. (*ISA*)

second DVD in the Definitive Edition. It is hoped that sometime in the future the film will be remastered as the quality on some DVD releases including the Blue-ray is rather poor.

Shown on British television (BBC 1) for the first time on 15 September, 1974 (five years to the day of its premiere), all the major television channels serving the UK (satellite included) have since broadcast *Battle of Britain*.

On Release

While it did not win any Oscars and in this day and age is often looked upon as just an ordinary film, it holds a special place in the hearts of aircraft enthusiasts the world over. It was an incredible achievement to gather so many 'real' vintage aircraft together just for a film. As aircraft films go it was indeed a milestone, which took a great deal of courage, skill and determination to make. Had it not been for the likes of Ben S. Fisz, Harry Saltzman, Guy Hamilton and Hamish Mahaddie, you would probably not be reading this book today.

As one 'kind' film critic of the day put it, "There will never be another aviation film quite like it".

Just one of countless articles appearing about the film in aviation enthusiast publications. (*PAC*)

Reel 13

Cast and Credits

Harry Saltzman and Ben Fisz did a remarkable job in assembling an all-star cast for *Battle of Britain*. The list of performers read like a veritable *Who's Who* of the British cinema, with big names such as Sir Laurence Olivier, Sir Ralph Richardson, Sir Michael Redgrave, Kenneth More, Michael Caine, Robert Shaw, Christopher Plummer, Patrick Wymark and Trevor Howard all making significant appearances throughout the film.

Lord Dowding, Commander-in-Chief of Fighter Command during the Battle of Britain, visits the film set. Group Captain Bader insisted on pushing the 'Old Man's' chair. Other technical advisors pictured are Air Commodore Al Deere (in check shirt), Wing Commander Robert Stanford Tuck (black tie), and to his left, Group Captain Johnny Kent; Lord Dowding is no doubt enjoying Susannah York's attention! (*PAC*)

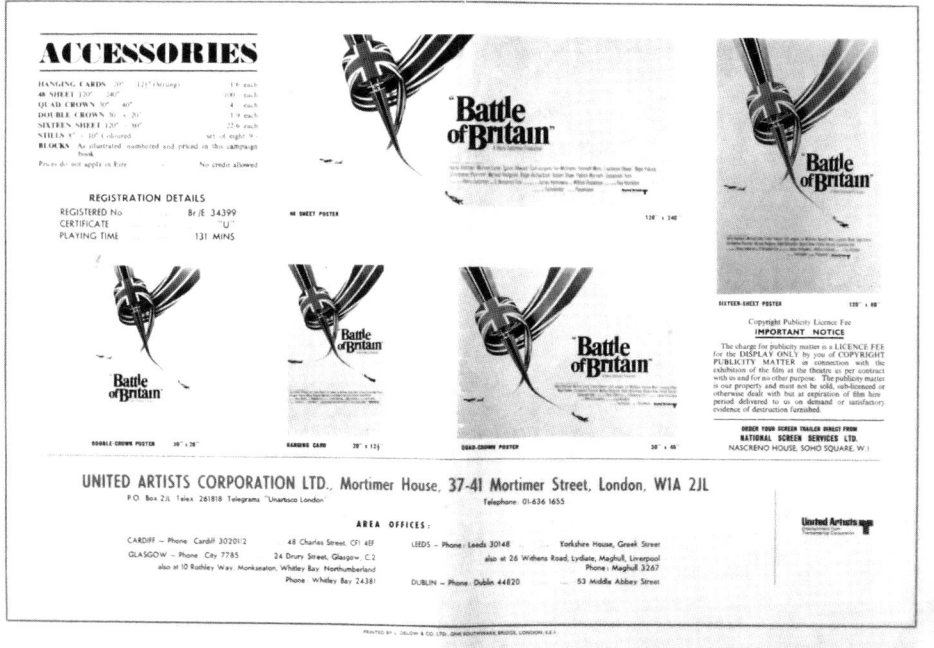

Publicity material available to cinemas via the Exhibitors Campaign Book. (*PAC*)

Some of the younger and lesser well-known members of the cast later went on to achieve screen stardom. Edward Fox became the sinister assassin in the film *Day of the Jackal*, and on the television screen he took the lead role as the Prince of Wales in the series *Edward and Mrs Simpson*.

Ian McShane appeared in a number of other films (*If It's Tuesday This Must Be Belgium* – 1969, *Villain* – 1971 and *Ransom* – 1974) before finding fame with his portrayal of the roguish antique dealer in the BBC television series *Lovejoy*. Barry Foster played the Dutch detective *Van der Valk* in the very successful ITV series during the early 1970s, and also appeared as the 'necktie murderer' in Alfred Hitchcock's 1972 film *Frenzy*.

Coming down the ladder of priority somewhat, actor John Savident only appeared in *Battle of Britain* for about one minute, uttering just a handful of lines in the process. He later went on to appear in several television costume dramas, as well as taking a leading role in the hugely popular ITV soap opera *Coronation Street*, in which he played the highly comical butcher, Fred Elliot. Behind the cameras was the cream of the British film industry. Director Guy Hamilton had a reputation for getting every detail right. His previous work on films such as *The African Queen*, *The Colditz Story*, *A Touch of Larceny* and the James Bond film *Goldfinger* had stood him in good stead for his work on *Battle of Britain*. Assistant Director Derek Cracknell had previously worked on *A Shot in the Dark*, *The Blue Max*, *Robbery* and *2001 A Space Odyssey*, before coming to *Battle of Britain*. He was later involved in the productions *Live and Let Die*, *Aces High*, *The Wild Geese*, *Evil Under the Sun*, *Supergirl* and *Aliens*.

Director of Photography Freddie Young's work on *The Winslow Boy*, *The Barretts of Wimpole Street*, *Soloman & Sheba*, *Lawrence of Arabia*, *Dr Zhivago* and *You Only Live Twice*, among others, had won him wide acclaim and many awards in the world of film. Aerial Cameraman Skeets Kelly entered the film industry as a junior assistant to Freddie Young at

Battle of Britain 'Susannah York Film Contest'! (PAC)

A veritable plethora of promotional items connected with the film were produced, including these jig-saws and FROG (Flies Right Off Ground) scale plastic model kits. (*PAC*)

the Elstree British & Dominion Studios. He made his name as an aerial cameraman on such films as *Sink the Bismarck*, *Those Magnificent Men in their Flying Machines* and The *Blue Max* before working on *Battle of Britain*. His life and career were cut short when he was killed in an accident during the filming of *Zeppelin* in 1970. Battle's other aerial cameraman, John Jordan, was also to lose his life during an aerial sequence for a film. Jordan fell out of a B-25 Mitchell bomber while shooting footage for *Catch 22* in 1969.

In front of, and behind, the cameras, *Battle of Britain* truly had an international star cast. The following is not intended to be a complete list but represents a large proportion of the many hundreds of individuals who made the film possible.

138 Battle of Britain: The Movie

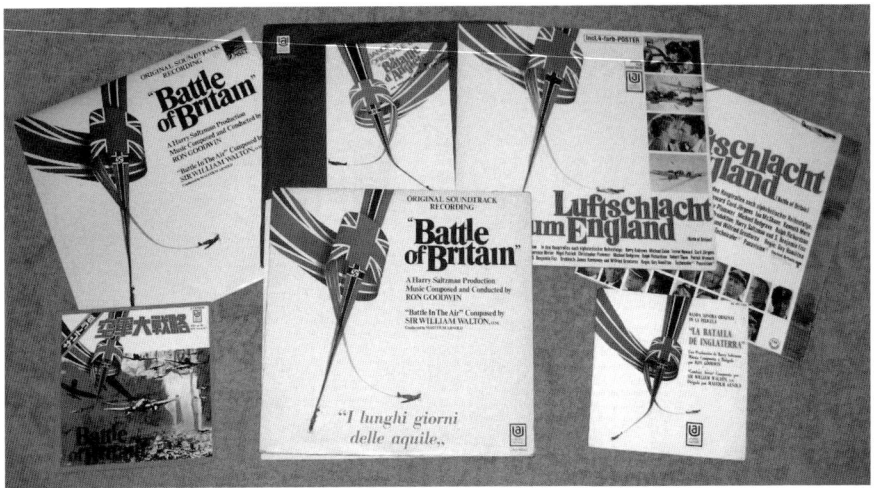

Vinyl movie score LP, posters and CDs. (*PAC*)

Plaistow Pictorial posters and postcards. (*PAC*)

Cast and Credits

Cast

General Theo Osterkamp	Wilfred van Aacken
Major Brandt, Heinkel Wing Leader	Alexander Allerson
Jeschonnek, Luftwaffe Chief of Staff	Karl Otto Alberty
Sir Francis Stokes, Under Secretary of State for Air	Harry Andrews
Aircraft Fitter Albert Farmer	Peter Angelis
Warrant Officer Warwick	John Bascomb
Andy's Wife	Michael Bates
Squadron Leader Canfield	Isla Blair
Willoughby's Assistant	Michael Caine
Policeman	Tom Chatto
Sergeant Pilot Jamie	John Comer
'B' Station Intelligence Officer	James Cosmo
'A' Station Plot Room Controller	Basil Dignam
Northolt Flight Commander	Eric Dodson
Wing Commander Willoughby	Michael Elwyn
Pilot	Robert Flemyng
Squadron Leader Edwards	Gareth Forward
Pilot Officer Archie	Barry Foster
Squadron Leader Tom Evans	Edward Fox
Feldmarschall Erhard Milch	W.G. Foxley
Sergeant Pilot Chris	Dietrich Frauboes
Feldmarschall Albert Kesselring	David Griffin
General Fink	Peter Hager
WAAF Corporal Seymour	Wolf Harnish
Bruno, Messerschmitt Pilot	Pat Heywood
Air Vice-Marshal Keith Park	Reinhard Horras
Peter	Trevor Howard
Brandt's navigator	Myles Hoyle
Baron Max von Richter	Alf Jungermann
Boehm	Curt Jurgens
Flight Sergeant Arthur	Helmut Kircher
Skipper's Wife	Duncan Lamont
Workman in Blitz	Sarah Lawson
Sergeant Pilot Andy	Reg Lye
	Ian McShane

140   Battle of Britain: The Movie

Battle of Britain bubble-gum included these cards which were avidly swapped and collected by enthusiastic school children. (*PAC*)

Pasco	Mark Malicz
Old Man in Church Hall	George Merrit
Peter's First New Boy	Richard Morant
British Embassy Valet	Richardson Morgan
Group Captain Baker	Kenneth More
French NCO	André Morell
Major Foehn	Paul Neuhaus
Air Minister	Anthony Nicholls
Air Chief Marshal Sir Hugh Dowding	Sir Laurence Olivier
Group Captain Hope	Nigel Patrick
Lady Kelly	Eileen Peel
Simon	Nicholas Pennell
Beppo Schmidt, Luftwaffe Intelligence Colonel	Malte Petzel
Squadron Leader Colin Harvey	Christopher Plummer
Falke, Senior Messerschmitt Pilot	Manfred Reddeman

Air Vice-Marshal Evill	Sir Michael Redgrave
'C' Squadron Pilot	Ben Richardson
David Kelly, British Minister in Switzerland	Sir Ralph Richardson
Reichsmarschall Herman Goering	Hein Riess
Senior Signals Officer Harley	John Savident
Ox	Andrzej Scibor
Squadron Leader Skipper	Robert Shaw
Adolf Hitler	Rolf Stiefel
'C' Squadron Pilot	Nicholas Tate
RAF Flight Sergeant	Reg Thomason
Sergeant Pilot Charlie Lambert	Alan Tucker
Lift Operator/MoD	Edward Williams
Jean Jaques	Jean Wladon
Air Vice-Marshal Trafford Leigh-Mallory	Patrick Wymark
WAAF Section Officer Maggie Harvey	Susannah York

Yet more publications… (*PAC*)

Books dedicated to the film: Leonard Moseley's 1968 book in hard and softback, and the late Robert Rudhall's original *Battle of Britain: The Movie* and *Battle of Britain Film: The Photo Album*, both published by Dilip Sarkar's former Ramrod Publications. (*PAC*)

Production Credits

Executive Producer	Harry Saltzman
Producer	Benjamin S. Fisz
Associate Producer	John Palmer
Director	Guy Hamilton
Assistant Director	David Bracknell
First Assistant Director	Derek Cracknell
Screenplay	James Kennaway
	Wilfred Greatorex
Director of Photography	Freddie Young BSC

Director of Photography (Second Unit)	Bob Huke BSC
Editor	Bert Bates
Sound Editors	James Shields
	Edward Mason
Music composed & conducted by	Ron Goodwin
'Battle in the Air' composed by	Sir William Walton OM
Conducted by	Malcolm Arnold
Chief Technical Advisor	G/C T.G Mahaddie
Technical & Tactical Advisors	G/C Tom Gleave
	W/C R. Stanford-Tuck
	W/C Robert Wright
	S/L James H. Lacey DFM
	S/L B. Drobinski
	W/C Claire Legge
German Technical & Tactical Advisors	Lt Gen Adolf Galland
	Col Hans Brustellin
	Major Franz Frodl

Lobby cards. (*PAC*)

Producer's Assistant	David Haft
Supervising Art Director	Maurice Carter GFAD
Assistant Art Directors	Alan Tomkins
	Bert Davey GFAD
	Tony Masters
	Lionel Couch
	Jack Maxstead
	Andrew Campbell

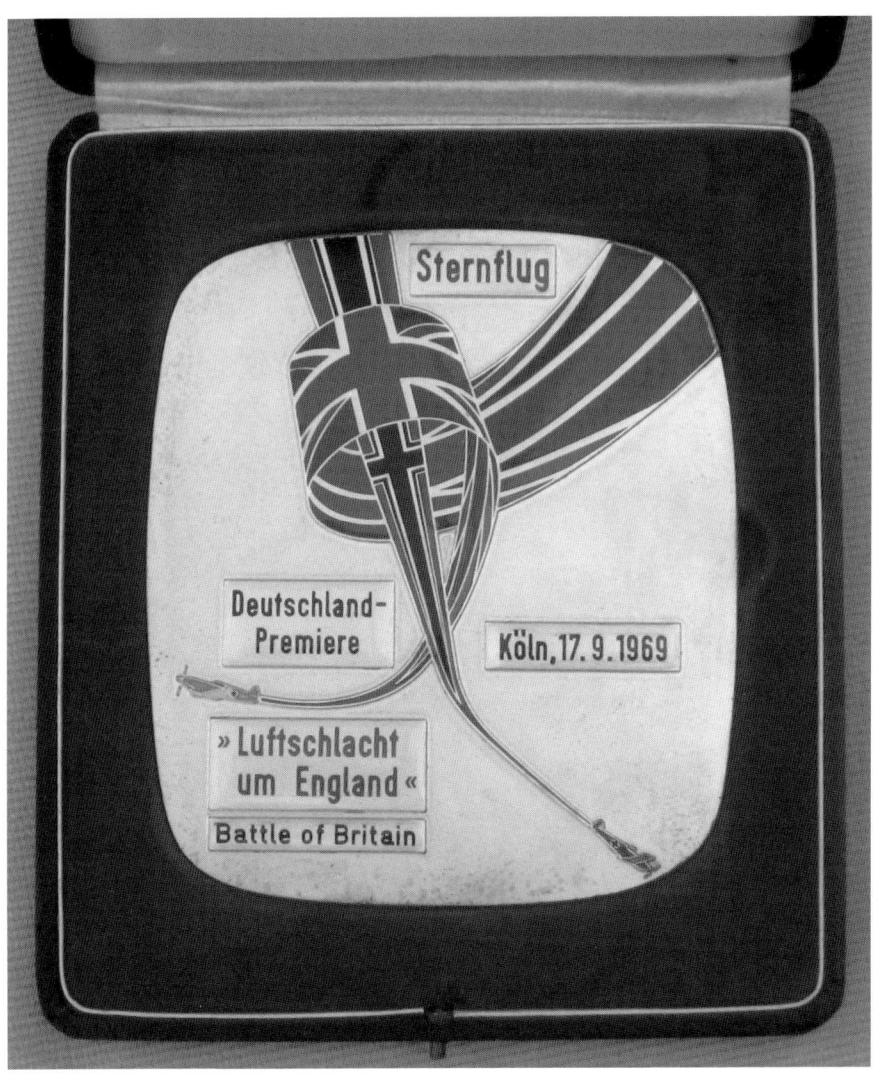

German premiere souvenir plaque. (*PAC*)

Cast and Credits

Buchon Yellow 10, Duxford. (*PAC*)

	William Hutchinson
	GFAD
	Tony Rimmington
	William Alexander
	Gill Parrondo
Camera Plane Pilot	John 'Jeff' Hawke
Camera Plane Co-Pilot	Duane Egli
Helicopter Pilot	John Crewdson
Camera Plane Modification	Robert E. Weimer
	Frank Hill
	Flying 'W' Products
	Hill Air Co
Aerial Unit Director	Quentin Lawrence
Aerial Photography	Skeets Kelly
	John Jordan
Special Effects Supervisor	Wally Veevers
Researcher	John Roast
MoD Airspace Supervisor (ATC)	W/C Leslie Young
Property Buyer	Ron Baker

Production Supervisor	John Palmer
Chief Production Accountant	Ron Allday
Unit Doctor (Spain)	Raphael Torroba
Replica Aircraft Construction Manager	Ken Softly
Production Office	Tony Smith
Properties Manager	John 'Paddy' Bennett
Props	John Chisholm
Publicity (USA)	Dick McKay
Chief Electrician	Vic Smith
Camera Operator	Dudley Lovell
Head of Publicity	Derek Coyte
Publicity Executive (in charge of liaison)	Air Cdr James Wallace
Publicity Assistant	Jill Thomas
Publicity Head Writer	Tom Hutchinson
Unit Publicity Director	John Willis
Head of Television Publicity	Christopher Doll
Radio Publicity	John Dyas
Model Effects Supervisor	John Siddal

Two-seater Spitfire TE308. (*PAC*)

Cast and Credits 147

Clapper-board. (*PAC*)

Model Unit Supervisor	Richard Conway
Radio Control Model Pilots	Mick Charles
	Chris Olsen
	David Platt
	Jack Morton
	A. Oliver
	J. Hoesli
	J. Holden
	J. Kirk
	T. Thomas
Replica Aircraft Effects	Ken King
	Les Steele
British Fighter Leader	W/C George Elliot
Spanish Air Force Leader	Comandante Pedro Santa Cruz
Sound	Gordon Everrett
	Gordon McCallum
Special Effects (Physical)	Cliff Richardson

148 Battle of Britain: The Movie

	Glenn Robinson
	John Richardson
	Nick Alder
	Wally Armitage
	Alan Barnard
	Jimmy Harris
	Garth Inns
	Roy Whybrow
Matte Effects	Wally Veevers
	Ray Caple
Optical Effects	Ronnie Wass
Production Supervisor	Sydney Streeter
Production Manager	Claud Hudson
Spanish Production Manager	Agustin Pastor
Production Manager (Aerial Unit)	Bernard Williams
Continuity	Elaine Schreyeck

Susannah York and Guy Hamilton with Lord Dowding, Squadron Leader 'Ginger' Lacey, Group Captain Douglas Bader and Wing Commander Bob Stanford Tuck. (*PAC*)

Cast and Credits 149

Press photo of 'Me 109s'. (*PAC*)

Casting Director	Maude Spector
Main Title Design	Maurice Binder
German Casting & Dialogue Director	Carl Fox-Duering
Carpenter	William Creighton
Wardrobe Manager	John Wilson-Apperson
Wardrobe Mistress	Brenda Dabbs
Hairdresser	A.G. Scott
Chief Make-up	George Frost
	Eric Allwright

Colour by Technicolor Filmed in Panavision © Spitfire Productions Limited Distributed By United Artists.

Feature from the *Worcester Evening News* promoting the film's arrical in the 'Faithful City'. (*Dilip Sarkar Archive [DSA]*)

A Schwarm of film 'Me 109s'. (*GBC*)

'Me 109s' prepare to take-off for a bomber escort mission from their 'French' airfield actually in Spain, 1968. (*GBC*)

Spitfire AR213 during filming. (*PAC*)

The film's aircraft often appeared wearing different code letters, providing the impression of more aircraft than there actually were. Codes were self-adhesive, not spray painted, and supplied by the 3M company. Here, Spitfire PR.XIX has its codes changed at Duxford. (*PAC*)

The Ju 52 transport used in the film. (*PAC*)

From left: 'Generalmajor Theo Osterkamp' (Wilfred von Aacken) and 'Reichsmarschall Hermann Göring (Hein Reiss) watching formations of Luftwaffe aircraft heading for England. (*PAC*)

Spitfires on patrol. (*PAC*)

Duxford's single-bay hangar being demolished for the film's airfield attack scene. (*PAC*)

'He 111s' London-bound. (*PAC*)

'Squadron Leader Skipper', played by Robert Shaw, who claimed to have based his character on the legendary South African ace 'AG 'Sailor' Malan. In truth, Malan was a softly-spoken but compelling leader, nothing like the aggressive martinet portrayed by Shaw, which was more like the legless ace Douglas Bader, Indeed, the connection between Shaw's character and Malan remains a disappointment to the ace's family. (*PAC*)

Aircrew and actors during filming at Duxford, 1968. (*JRC*)

'Heinkels!' (*JRC*)

Damage to a replica Hurricane. (*JRC*)

Hurricanes and Spitfires patrolling for the cameras. (*JRC*)

In 1968, Michael Dodsworth was a young Civil Servant working at Manston airfield, one of the film's locations, and well-placed, therefore, to photograph this unique array of aircraft operating from this former Battle of Britain airfield. Here we have Me 109 Buchons lined up. (*Michael Dodsworth Collection* [*hereafter acknowledged as MDC*])

Yellow 12 at Manston. (*MDC*)

Red-nosed Me 109 Buchon at Manston. (*MDC*)

Michael Dodsworth was lucky enough to be shown inside a CASA at Manson in 1968. (*MDC*)

CASA111 at Manston. (*MDC*)

Buchon cockpit, Manston 1968. (*MDC*)

CASA 111 nose close-up, Manston, 1968. (*MDC*)

CASA 111, Manston. (*MDC*)

Hurricane LF653 undergoing maintenance at Manston. (*MDC*)

Hurricane LF653, Manston. (*MDC*)

Squadron Leader David Spink, Officer Commanding Standards Squadron at RAF Linton-on-Ouse, flew Spitfires and Hurricanes during the filming. (*JRC*)

For some time prior to the film's release there was a veritable promotional barrage of media articles and collectables, amongst the latter this postcard album comprising film stills. (*PAC*)

The die-cast model company Dinky produced a Spitfire and Stuka associated with the film – now highly prized and collectable items. (*PAC*)

The film's iconic poster. (*PAC*)

The Japanese release's poster. (*PAC*)

Cover of an Exhibitors Campaign Book. (*PAC*)

Battle of Britain was launched at London's Dominion Theatre on, appropriately, Battle of Britain Day, 15 September 1969. Lord Dowding, Commander in Chief of Fighter Command in 1940, and many of The Few were invited to the premiere – this is the brochure and tickets of Wing Commander Roger Boulding, who flew Spitfires during the summer of 1940 with Squadron Leader 'Sailor' Malan's famous 74 'Tiger' Squadron. (*DSA*)

Front cover of the film's brochure. (*DSA*)

The premiere's after show party invitation of Wing Commander Bernard 'Jimmy' Jennings AFC DFM, who flew Spitfires with 19 Squadron in the Duxford Sector during the Battle of Britain. (*DSA*)

From inside the brochure belonging to Dilip Sarkar, signed by composer Ron Goodwin and many of The Few at the launch of the original *Battle of Britain: The Movie* at Worcester Guildhall in 2000. (*DSA*)

Reel 14

The Aircraft Fleet, Then and Now

The main British aircraft type used in the film was the Supermarine Spitfire. A round dozen were able to fly for the cameras, while seven were brought up to taxying status. The remaining seven were used as static dressing. All of these airframes came to the film from a host of different locations, far and wide. Most of the fighters still survive today and are spread throughout the world.

Spitfire taxiing whilst airfield is 'bombed'. (*John Rush Collection* [*JRC*])

Over the ensuing years a myth has been perpetuated regarding the two-seat Spitfires used in the production. Several previous accounts of the filming have stated that Spitfire Tr.8 MT818 (G-AIDN), the prototype two-seat variant of the famous fighter, was used by the film company. As has been mentioned elsewhere in this book, the two examples of Spitfire trainers utilised during the filming were both Tr.9s. At the time of the making of *Battle of Britain*, G-AIDN was owned and flown by John S. Fairey, the younger son of Sir Richard Fairey, founder of the Fairey Aviation Company.

Despite what has been suggested in the past, G-AIDN was probably the only airworthy Spitfire in Europe not to take part in the film. In 1999 John Fairey recalled the reasons why: "Hamish Mahaddie made several approaches to lease the aircraft, but due to one reason or another we could not agree on a suitable set of terms and conditions for the aircraft to be used by the film company. I remember a few years later when I sold the

Film and air crews at Duxford, 1968. (*JRC*)

aircraft, I was very tempted to offer it as 'The only Spitfire not to be used in the *Battle of Britain* film', just as a bit of a sales gimmick."

Of the entire Spanish Air Force fleet of 32 Heinkel 111s utilised, sadly very few are left today, the vast majority of the bombers being scrapped in the 1970s. Spitfire Productions secured some 27 Hispano Buchons, and six Hawker Hurricanes brought up the rear in terms of airframe numbers used. Virtually all of the latter two types are still extant.

Spitfire

Mark/Identity	Pre-Film Location/Status	Film	Present Location/Status
Ia AR213 (G-AIST)	Old Warden/Stored	A (Airworthy)	Spitfire the One Ltd Duxford. Airworthy
IIa P7350 (G-AWIJ)	RAF Colerne Museum, Static	A	BBMF, RAF Coningsby, Airworthy
Vb AB910 (G-AISU)	BBMF, RAF Coltishall, Airworthy	A	BBMF, RAF Coningsby, Airworthy
Vb BL614	RAF Credenhill, Gate Guard	T (Taxi)	RAF Museum Hendon, Displayed
Vb BM597	RAF Church Fenton. Gate Guard	R (Replica)	Historic Aircraft Collection, Duxford airworthy (G-MKVB).
Vb EP120	RAF Boulmer, Gate Guard	S (Static)	The Fighter Collection, Duxford, Airworthy (G-LFVB)
Vc AR501 (G-AWII)	Shuttleworth Collection, Fuselage displayed	A	Shuttleworth Collection, Old Warden,
IX MH415 (G-AVDJ)	Rousseau Aviation, France	A	Care of Air Leasing, Sywell UK
	Stored Warbirds Flight Club Pty Ltd		Under restoration to airworthy
IX MH434 (G-ASJV)	Tim Davies, Elstree, Airworthy	A	Old Flying Machine Company, Duxford, Airworthy
IX MK297 (G-ASSD)	CAP, Swanton Morley, Stored	A	Destroyed in CWH hangar fire, Hamilton, 1993 (N9BL)
IX MK356	RAF Locking, Gate Guard	S	BBMF, RAF Coningsby, Airworthy
Tr.IX MJ772 (G-AVAV)	Tony Samuelson, Elstree, Airworthy	A	Warbird Experiences Biggin Hill, Airworthy
Tr.IX TE308 (G-AWGB)	Irish Air Corps, Baldonnel, Airworthy	A	Warbird Experiences Biggin Hill, Airworthy
XIV RM689 (G-ALGT)	Roll-Royce, Hucknall, Airworthy	A	Crash remains stored with Rolls-Royce

Mark/Identity	Pre-Film Location/Status	Film	Present Location/Status
XVIe RW382	RAF Leconfield, Gate Guard	S	Downlock Ltd Biggin Hill Airworthy (G-XVIA)
XVIe SL574	RAF Bentley Priory, Gate Guard	S	San Diego Aerospave Museum, USA, Displayed
XVIe SM411	RAF Wattisham, Gate Guard	T	Polish National Museum, Krakow, Displayed
XVIE TB382	RAF Hospital Ely, Gate Guard	T	Airframe Assemblies I.O.W. Stored
XVIe TE311	RAF Tangmere, Gate Guard	T	BBMF, RAF Coningsby, (Airworthy)
XVIe TE356	RAF Bicester, Gate Guard	T	Biggin Hill Heritage Hangar. Stored
XVIe TE384	RAF Syerston, Gate Guard	T	Ken McBride, California, USA, Stored
XVIe TE476	RAF Neatishead, Gate Guard	T	Fantasy of Flight Museum, Florida, USA, displayed (N476TE)
PR.XIX PM631	BBMF, RAF Coltishall, Airworthy	A	BBMF, RAF Coningsby, Airworthy
PR.XIX PM651	RAF Benson, Gate Guard	S	RAF Museum Reserve Collection, RAF Cosford, Stored
PR.XIX PS853	BBMF, RAF Coltishall, Airworthy	A	Rolls-Royce Plc, East Midlands Airport, Airworthy (G-RRGN)
PR.XIX PS915	RAF Leuchars, Gate Guard	S	BBMF, RAF Coningsby, Airworthy
F.2I LA198	187 ATC Sqn, Worcester	S	Kelvingrove Museum Glasgow displayed

Along with those included in the main list, several additional Spitfire airframes were allocated to Spitfire Productions Ltd, but never appeared in the film. Some of these following aircraft were utilised for spares in order to keep the airworthy serviceable.

Spitfire 'Extras'

Mark/Identity	Pre-Film Location/Status	Film Status	Present Location/Status
Ia K9942	RAF Bicester, RAF Ex Flt	Spares back-up	RAF Museum Cosford. Displayed
XIV NH904	Bunny Brooks Garage, Hoylake, Static	Spares back-up	Planes of Fame Museum East, Palm Springs, California, USA, Displayed
XIV RM694	Manchester Tankers Ltd, Lancs, Stored	Spares back-up	Biggin Hill Heritage Hangar. Stored

The Aircraft Fleet, Then and Now

Mark/Identity	Pre-Film Location/Status	Film Status	Present Location/Status
XVIe TB863	Pinewood Film Studios, Stored	Spares back-up	Temora Air Museum Australia. Airworthy (VH-XVI)
XVIe TE184	Royton ATC, Gate Guard	Spares back-up	Stephen Stead oprated in Europe Airworthy (G-MXVI)
F.21 LA226	RAF Little Rissington, Gate Guard	Spares back-up	RAF Museum Reserve Collection, RAF Cosford, Stored
F.24 PK724	RAF Gaydon, Gate Guard	Spares back-up	RAF Museum, Hendon, Displayed

Hawker Hurricane

Mark/Identity	Pre-Film Location/Status	Film Status	Present Location/Status
I P2617	RAF Bicester, Exhibition Flight	Transferred to Henlow for the film but not used.	RAF Museum, Hendon, Static
Ib Z7015	Shuttleworth Collection, Static (Sea Hurricane)	T	Shuttleworth Collection, G-BK TH, Airworthy
IIc LF363	BBMF, RAF Coltishall, Airworthy	A	BBMF, RAF Coningsby, Airworthy
IIc LF751	RAF Bentley Priory, Gate Guard	Mould for film	RAF Manston History Museum, Static replicas
IIc PZ865 (G-AMAU)	Hawker Siddeley, Dunsfold, Airworthy	A	BBMF, RAF Coningsby, Airworthy
XII RCAF 5377/CF-SMI (G-AWLW)	Robert Diemert, Canada, Airworthy	A	Destroyed in CWH hangar fire, Hamilton 1993 (C-GCWH)

Messerschmitt Bf 109/Hispano HA 1112 M1L Buchon

Mark/Identity	Pre-Film Location/Status	Film Status	Present Location/Status
C4K-30	Spanish Air Force, Tablada	Spares	Air Leasing Sywell UK Awaiting restoration
C4K-31/G-AWHE	Spanish Air Force, Tablada	A	Air Fighter Academy Heringsorf Germany
C4K-61/G-AWHF	Spanish Air Force, Tablada	A	Restoration Germany
C4K-75/G-AWHG	Spanish Air Force, Tablada	A	Undergoing repair after accident Germany
C4K-99/G-AWHM	Spanish Air Force, Tablada	A	Meier Motors Germany
C4K-100/G-AWHJ	Spanish Air Force, Tablada	A	Kalamazoo Aviation Museum, USA
C4K-102/G-AWHK	Spanish Air Force, Tablada	A	Aircraft Restoration Company Duxford UK

Mark/Identity	Pre-Film Location/Status	Film Status	Present Location/Status
C4K-105/G-AWHH	Spanish Air Force, Tablada	A	Anglia Aircraft Restorations Sywell UK
C4K-106/G-AWHI	Spanish Air Force, Tablada	A	In store Salinas USA
C4K-107	Spanish Air Force, Tablada	T	Old Flying Machine Company, G-BOML, Crashed Spain, 25/9/99, written off, scrapped
C4K-111	Spanish Air Force, Tablada	Studio Filming	Air Leasing Sywell UK under restoration
C4K-112/G-AWHC	Spanish Air Force, Tablada	A (two-seat)	Air Leasing Sywell UK

Messerschmitt Bf 109/Hispano HA 1112 M4L Buchon

C4K-114	Spanish Air Force, Tablada	Spares	Aviation & Space Museum, Rockcliffe
C4K-121	Spanish Air Force, Tablada	T	Texas Air Museum, USA, Rebuild
C4K-122/G-AWHL	Spanish Air Force, Tablada	A	Museum of Flight, Seattle, USA
C4K-126/G-AWHD	Spanish Air Force, Tablada	A	In store Salinas USA
C4K-127/G-AWHO	Spanish Air Force, Tablada	A	EAA Museum, Oshkosh, USA
C4K-130/G-AWHN	Spanish Air Force, Tablada	A	Erickson Aircraft Collection USA
C4K-131	Spanish Air Force, Tablada	T	Eric Vormezeele, Belgium
C4K-134	Spanish Air Force, Tablada	T	Wittmundhafen AB Museum, Static
C4K-135	Spanish Air Force, Tablada	T	Air Fighter Academy Heringsdorf Germany
C4K-144/G-AWHP	Spanish Air Force, Tablada	A	Destroyed in fatal accident, CAF Texas, 19/12/1987
C4K-152/G-AWHR	Spanish Air Force, Tablada	A	Legendary Aircraft Hungary
C4K-154	Spanish Air Force, Tablada	Spares	In store awaiting rebuild
C4K-169/G-AWHT	Spanish Air Force, Tablada	A	Flugmuseum Messerschmitt Manching, Germany
C4K-170/G-AWHS	Spanish Air Force, Tablada	A	Auto & Technik Museum, Sinsheim. Germany, Static
C4K-172	Spanish Air Force, Tablada	T	Cavanaugh Flight Museum, Dallas, USA

Heinkel 111 /CASA 2111

Although the entire Spanish Air Force complement of 32 Heinkels was utilised in the filming, it has often been said that better use could have been made of them in the finished film. Post filming, the Spaniards retired the remaining Heinkels and put them up for sale. Sadly, the then high asking price of around $6,500 (a mere drop in the ocean in prices of vintage aircraft these days) proved to be too much and few buyers came forward. Hence, the bulk of the fleet was scrapped, with only a few being saved for future preservation.

It is without doubt that all of the world's surviving Spanish Heinkels almost certainly 'starred' in the film, and with this criteria the following list includes those currently extant airframes. B=Medium Bomber, BR=Bomber/Reconnaissance, T8=Command Transport/Dual Control Trainer.

CASA 2111s In Preservation:

Identity	Pre-Film Location	Status	Present Location/Status
BR.21-14	Spanish Air Force, Tablada	A	Flugausstellung Museum Hermeskeil Germany
BR.21-129	Spanish Air Force, Tablada	A	Musée de l'Air, Paris, France, Stored
B.21-27	Spanish Air Force, Tablada	A	Cavanaugh Flight Museum, Dallas, USA
BR.21-37	Spanish Air Force, Tablada	A	Flying Heritage Collection Everett USA
B.21-77	Spanish Air Force, Tablada	A	Deutsches Museum Schleissheim Germany
B.21-82	Spanish Air Force, Tablada	A	Technik Museum, Sinsheim, Germany
B.21-39	Spanish Air Force, Tablada	A	Arlington USA stored
T.8B-97	Spanish Air Force, Tablada	A	Museo del Aire, Tablada, Spain, Stored
Identity	Pre-Film Location	Status	Present Location/Status
B21-103	Spanish Air Force, Tablada	A	Kent Battle of Britain Museum UK
B21-117	Spanish Air Force, Tablada	A	Gatow Germany stored
B21-29	Spanish Air Force, Tablada	A	USAF Museum, Dayton, USA, stored
BR21-20	Spanish Air Force Tablada	S	Studio filming fuselage; Austria under restoration

Unfortunately, none of the Heinkels used in the film are in airworthy condition. The last airworthy example, the Arizona Wing of the Confederate Air Force's T.8B-124 (N72615) was lost in a fatal crash in 2003.

Out of the survivors it seems unlikely that any will be restored to flight in the near future. The Dallas-based Cavanaugh Flight Museum's example could be returned to flight given an extensive examination and overhaul, the airframe was purchased from the EdA (Spanish Airforce) by Doug Arnold's Warbirds of Great Britain collection at Blackbushe, in the mid-1970s before being exported to the USA. Initially on display at the Wings and Wheels Museum at Orlando, Florida, it eventually passed into the hands of David Tallichet's Military Aircraft Restoration Corp and moved to Chino, California. After spending several years dormant at Chino, it was ferried down to Texas in 1996 after a spell residing at Topeka's Combat Air Museum, Kansas. The aircraft is maintained in excellent condition but is on static display.

Lord Dowding sits in on a film aircrew briefing. (*JRC*)

They Also Served

Battle of Britain also utilised several other aircraft in minor roles, in front of and behind the cameras. A pair of Spanish Air Force Junkers Ju 52 (CASA 352) tri-motor transports were used, one in Luftwaffe colours, for the opening title sequence and another during the Berlin scene. Both of these aircraft may still be in existence as a good number of Spanish Junkers' have survived. Not appearing in front of the cameras, Sud SA 318C Alouette II helicopter G-AWAP was used for much of the air to ground filming as well as a 'launch platform' for some of the models which were crashed or blown up during the shooting. Operated by the Helicopter Hire Company the aircraft was flown by the renowned movie pilot John Crewdson. G-AWAP was used on a number of other film projects, the Alouette crashed on Gat Sand in The Wash on 26 June 1983, tragically killing Crewdson and three observers on board. G-AWAP was eventually cancelled from the British Civil Aircraft Register as destroyed on 11 July 1984.

In the early days of the project the Ministry of Defence made available its Heinkel IIIH-20 701152, Junkers Ju 87G-2 494083, Junkers Ju 88R-1 360043 and Messerschmitt Bf 109G-2 10639 (the later eventually becoming the famous airworthy *Black Six* G-USTV), but with the advent of the Spanish 'Luftwaffe' these genuine German aircraft were not used. However the JU87 Stuka was ground run and its engine note was recorded.

Three complete Percival Proctors were purchased – G-AIAE, P6227 (G-AIEY) and LZ589 (G-ALOK) – along with the fuselage of G-AIED. As related in the main text, Vivian Bellamy converted two of the Proctors to Stuka 'lookalikes'. Only G-AIEY actually flew, but it was not used in the film. At the end of filming all three Proctors were reportedly acquired by John Hawke. Subsequently put into storage, it is believed that the trio was eventually scrapped, although one featured as a crashed aircraft in the 1974 Spike Milligan Film *Adolf Hitler My Part in His Downfall*.

The gathering together of all these airframes and their subsequent disposal throughout the world gave the historic aircraft preservation movement a significant kick-start, and undoubtedly led to the increase of interest in restoring and flying former Second World War combat aircraft. Thus the global warbird movement we have and enjoy today can really be traced back to Saltzman and Fisz's 'Private Air Force'.

160 Battle of Britain: The Movie

Buchons at Manston, 1968. (*Michael Dodsworth Collection* [*MDC*])

The Aircraft Fleet, Then and Now

The Aircraft Fleet, Then and Now 163

Reel 15

The Big and 'Fantastic' Story: Battle of Britain in Context

In this whole new section, replacing his chapter entitled 'Just How Historically Accurate was Battle of Britain?', historian Dilip Sarkar provides a fascinating overview contextualising the 1969 epic, and a new 'reading' of the film.

For historians, the matter of history on film is often difficult and emotive. Translating the 'big story' to a couple of hours of cinema time, however, is a far from easy or straightforward task for film-makers – and the Battle of Britain, the high point of national consciousness and a multi-phased aerial conflict lasting sixteen weeks, is a big story indeed. Undertaking such a task is a huge responsibility, to be sure, because countless people learn their 'history' from popular culture and mass media. To them, film is a truism, a mirror, perhaps, reflecting the actual past. This cinematic 'reality', though, is a construct, a mythical presentation always underpinned by wider political, propaganda or commercial factors. Indeed, such broader influences have governed every representation of the Battle of Britain on film, whether during the Second World War or since – and by 1969, when *Battle of Britain* was screened, a great deal had changed since that totemic year of 1940.

In the immediate post-war period, many survivors, especially famous war heroes or those involved in particularly heroic operations, wrote and published their memoirs, or arranged for professional writers to do so. There was, it seemed, an insatiable demand by the British public to learn more of and perhaps better understand this global conflict, and great interruption to daily life through which they had lived. By the 1950s, the British film industry had also responded to popular demand, successfully transferring some of these inspirational stories to cinema screens – foremost amongst potential subjects being the Battle of Britain.

CASA 111s at Manston. (*MDC*)

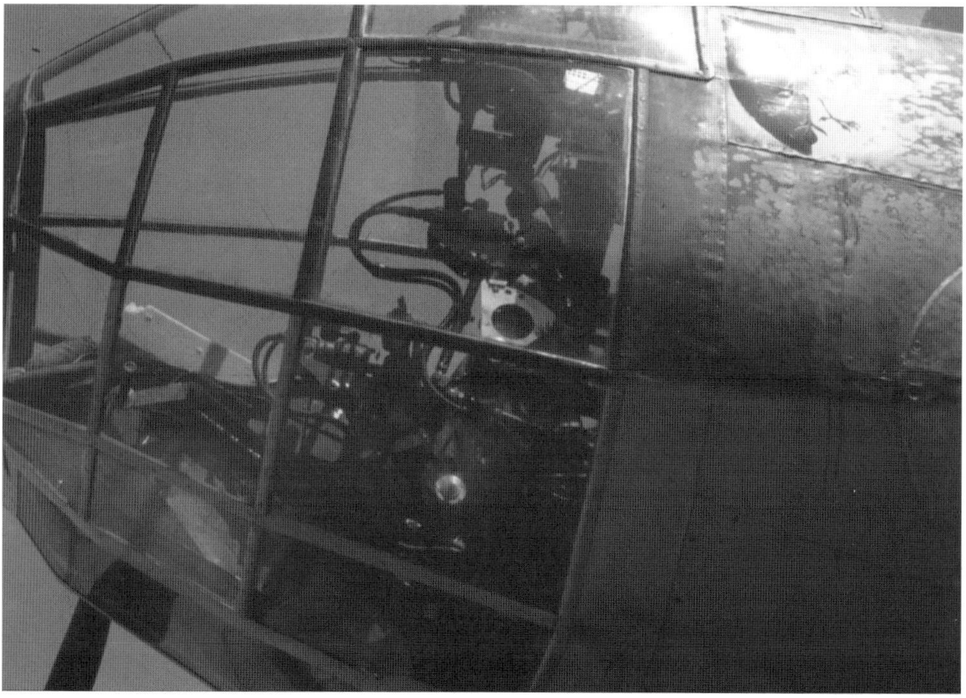

166 Battle of Britain: The Movie

The Big and 'Fantastic' Story: Battle of Britain in Context 167

This was, of course, a time still close to the actual event, and the RAF enthusiastically reminded the nation of what was recognised as its decisive victory, through annual open days and air shows at RAF bases, flypasts and commemorative services. Little wonder, then, that filmmakers considered the subject a potentially lucrative one.

In June 1951, work began on a film originally entitled *Battle of Britain*, but which was ultimately released as *Angels One Five*. This, however, was no attempt to deal with the 'big story'. Instead, the film focussed upon the story of Pilot Officer 'Sceptic' Baird, played by John Gregson, a new arrival on 'Pimpernel' Squadron, flying Hurricanes in the Battle of Britain. The film was well-received by newspaper reviewers and was a box-office success, although some film critics were lukewarm – Patrick Gibbs of the *Daily Telegraph* suggesting that it was too soon to bring the Battle of Britain to the cinema, on the grounds that 'it hangs now too uncertainly between memory and history'.

Nonetheless, several of the Few had attended the premier, including the sceptical legless air ace Group Captain Douglas Bader, who emerged stating that 'I came out amazed. I can't fault it in any detail'. The film was certainly popular with the public, and, as Josh Billings remarked in his annual survey of Britain's box-office statistics, had 'made a packet of money'. And that was what made the cameras reels go round.

In March 1954, the Australian former Spitfire pilot and journalist Paul Brickhill published *Reach for the Sky*, his authorised biography of Douglas Bader. The book was a massive success, selling hundreds of thousands of copies. Unsurprisingly, this clearly being an exceptional commercial commodity, film rights were quickly snapped up. Lewis Gilbert and Daniel Angel rapidly set-to, casting Kenneth More in the starring role, the resulting film being released to wide and popular acclaim during the summer of 1956.

The film, also called *Reach for the Sky*, completely dominated the box-office for the rest of that year – Billings concluding that it had been a 'colossal money-maker'. Although to a degree the events of 1940 and 1941 concerned much of the film, and were to some extent narrated and explained, *Reach for the Sky* was still no attempt to tell the 'big story'. This remained another film firmly focussed on an individual's story framed by wider events. One thing, however, was certain, during what was the golden age of British war films: the Battle of Britain was a money-spinner.

One notable thing about 1950s British war films, and *Angels One Five* and *Reach for the Sky* are no exceptions, is that it remained unthinkable to show the Germans in any kind of positive or sympathetic light. Bravely, Roy Ward Baker had directed *The One That Got Away*, which, released in 1957, was based on the book of that name by James Leasor and Kendal Burt, telling the story of Oberleutnant Franz von Werra. Von Werra was an enemy fighter pilot shot down and captured during the Battle of Britain and who infamously became the only German prisoner of war to escape from Allied custody and return home.

Baker was heavily criticised for heroicising a German airman. Nonetheless, his film was popular in both Britain and West Germany, making a profit of £3 million. Moreover, in 1956, a former Luftwaffe fighter ace currently serving in an RAF squadron on an exchange visit through NATO, was not allowed to take part in that year's annual Battle of Britain flypast over London. That same year, the Foreign Office had expressed concerns that the German war trophies displayed annually at Horse Guards could offend the democratic West Germans, who were a valued Cold War ally. Four years later, this commemoration was discontinued, and in 1961, the annual RAF flypast was scaled right back. Clearly, things were changing, the old 'triumphal mood', as the *Daily Express* put it, evaporating – and with it, potentially, the opportunity to translate *the Battle of Britain*'s big story to the silver screen.

By the 1960s, times had very much changed in post-war Britain. The domestic television was making a significant impact, a negative one so far as British cinema was concerned; the population increasingly watching the 'box' at home, rather than go to the 'flicks'. With reduced cinema attendance, the British film industry suffered financially. Indeed, from now on, the world of film would be dominated by America, and in Hollywood there was little or no interest in Britain's Finest Hour.

Moreover, by 1960, twenty years after the event and fifteen after the Second World War ended, there were generations of young people with no personal experience of what was seen as their parents' war, with which most modern teenagers had little or no affinity. Indeed, they actively sought to distance themselves from their parents' world and values, and, owing to the fear of nuclear weapons and America's controversial war in Vietnam, the decade saw a growing and vocal peace movement.

Hurricanes and Spitfires at Manston, 1968. (*MDC*)

The Big and 'Fantastic' Story: Battle of Britain in Context

172 Battle of Britain: The Movie

The Big and 'Fantastic' Story: Battle of Britain in Context

Also, in 1940, Britain had been head of its Empire and Commonwealth, the product of years of imperialism, but by now this had all but withered on the vine. India, that jewel in the crown, had been granted independence in 1947, starting the long process of decolonisation for other Empire states. In 1948, the British Nationality Act granted British citizenship to subjects of the British Commonwealth, providing an 'open door' policy to immigration, leading to mass post-war immigration into Britain from former British colonies. Britain's identity, therefore, was fundamentally changing, from being a superpower to a vassal of America, and internally dealing with the new age of multiculturalism. In short, the world and internal order had changed – and some did not now see the Battle of Britain as a big story to trumpet, but one best buried and forgotten.

Fortunately, the former RAF pilot and successful Polish film producer Ben Fisz was not amongst them. Fisz, together with his Director, Guy Hamilton, was determined to 'tell it how it was' and produce 'a tribute to the Few'. Both were aware of their self-set task's enormity – an even greater undertaking than most realise, perhaps, against the backdrop of the 'Swinging Sixties'.

In more recent times, however, various academic historians, not least amongst them Clive Ponting (*The Myth of 1940*) and Angus Calder (*The Myth of the Blitz*), have argued that the 'Finest Hour' was nothing of the sort and little more than a manufactured myth, something explored in detail by Malcolm Smith in his excellent study *Britain and 1940: History, Myth and Popular Memory*, and who wrote that 1940 and the Battle of Britain seems 'to have been the one genuinely heroic moment in twentieth-century British history. Britain was fighting alone against something which simply had to be stopped if any kind of acceptable values were to survive in Europe'. Guy Hamilton certainly acknowledged that 1940 was undoubtedly heavily myth-laden – but took a very different tack, one which this author wholeheartedly supports – proclaiming that his intention was 'to destroy the myth, only to create a greater myth, because it's a *fantastic* story'.

Although upon release in 1969, the American financed and British made *Battle of Britain* failed to excite the critics or aspire to investors' box-office expectations, there is no doubt that Fisz and Hamilton tried their best, under often difficult wider circumstances, to tell this '*fantastic* story', and, for the first – and probably last – time, succeeded in telling the big story that the Battle of Britain most certainly is.

Unlike previous films lauding individuals, Fisz and Hamilton showed the disparity between the politicians' agendas and Fighter Command's requirements, and touched upon the internal argument over strategy and tactics (more of which later). The contribution of foreign aircrew was not ignored, and neither was the WAAF. The suffering of civilians, work of the emergency services and Observer Corps (OC), along with the contribution made by radar, is all included. Bravely, the Germans, twelve years after Baker was criticised for *The One That Got Away*, were shown as a brave and skilled adversary, although the portly and flamboyant Luftwaffe chief and Hitler's deputy, Hermann Göring, rightly, was not portrayed so sympathetically. To aviation enthusiasts the world over, though, what made – and still makes – the film unique was the extensive use of actual aircraft, and brilliantly filmed and edited aerial sequences, married to a superb soundtrack by Sir William Walton and Ron Goodwin. Unlike *Angels One Five* and *Reach for the Sky*, it was also in full technicolour, making it more contemporary to modern audiences.

Just how historically accurate the film is, however, is not an easy question to answer, for it is a complex one. At the film's press conference, Battle of Britain ace Squadron Leader James 'Ginger' Lacey, who had worked as a Technical Advisor on the project, claimed that *Battle of Britain* was a catalogue of no less than 193 errors. Some were unavoidable and dictated by the availability of aircraft types and flying kit, for example, but clearly an effort was made to align these things as closely as practically possible with the real deal. These are, in any case, arguably micro details unaffecting the overall story-telling and end result, and noticed only by we enthusiasts.

On the macro stage there are certain things not quite right, or correctly interpreted and presented. Without question, however, the producers of *Battle of Britain* have left behind a rich legacy, and have done this big and '*fantastic* story' a great and lasting service.

The following are notes made during my 'reading' of Battle of Britain for this chapter, and cover the main and salient points, as I see them having watched the film countless times and studied the actual events involved for a lifetime.

The Big and 'Fantastic' Story: Battle of Britain in Context

Squadron Leader Lacey and Group Captain Townsend get reacquainted with a Spitfire. (*DSA*)

176 Battle of Britain: The Movie

Battle of Britain: A New 'Reading' of the film.

The film is of 2 hours and 12 minutes duration, so relevant times are shown in minutes and seconds preceding those figures.

00:28/2:12   In the opening few minutes, we have a clear message: the Fall of France is underway, Allied forces in full retreat. British soldiers in a (post-war) armoured car ponderously make their way West, towards the Channel coast, in a long, rag-taggle, column of French dejected civilians – now refugees. Overhead, an RAF Hawker Hurricane performs a victory roll before landing at an adjacent airfield. There we meet 'Harvey' (Christopher Plummer), a flight lieutenant and flight commander now leading his squadron after the CO, 'Jumbo', was reported missing. Harvey, however, takes issue with the victory roll just performed by 'Jamie', the latter having naively considered the low-level aerobatics a morale-boosting gesture for the refugees' benefit. Harvey is unmoved, making clear the value of both aircraft – and pilot.

01:44/2:12   Then, as a section of Hurricanes arrives, enter Robert Shaw's character, a comparatively elderly, bullish, no-nonsense squadron commander called 'Skipper'. According to Leonard Mosley in his 1969 book *Battle of Britain*, which accompanied the film's release, Shaw was apparently inspired by, and researched, the story of the legendary South African, AG 'Sailor' Malan, basing 'Skipper' on him. If this truly was Shaw's aim, it was a failure. Having written Malan's most recent biography, Malan, a pre-war pilot on 74 'Tiger' Squadron, who acceded to command that unit during the Battle of Britain, was a quiet, reserved and almost shy individual. A consummate professional, yes, presented as a cold-hearted killer on occasions by the propagandists, a loud-mouthed bullying martinet like 'Skipper', definitely not. The Malan family remain unhappy with the portrayal for these reasons, and Shaw's character appears more aligned to the irascible, swashbuckling, Douglas Bader than Malan.

02:30/2:12   Also, whilst in France, we have a clear indication of how society and the services were hierarchical and delineated by class and rank. At the time, only those with a public-school background, a School Certificate 'A' and a letter of recommendation signed by at least a colonel, were eligible to be commissioned. So, here we have the clearly 'posh' 'Pilot Officer Archie' (Edward Fox), sneeringly translating French for his companion, 'Sergeant-Pilot Andy' (Ian McShane, whose surname we learn later is 'Moore') who, by virtue of rank, has not the benefit of a private education, which in those days was the key to the primary professions. Nonetheless, 'Andy', with at least a grammar school education, throws the light-hearted put-down right back by translating himself 'Archam can't believe Sedan has fallen. I can'. After the disconcerting news from a French pilot that the Germans 'Will be 'ere in 'arf an hour', the Hurricanes hurriedly take-off, leaving the groundcrew to destroy the 'lame ducks' – just in time, as a formation of 'Me 109s' streaks across the airfield at zero-feet, strafing as they go.

05:57/2:12   The scene then abruptly changes to an Air Ministry corridor, where we meet Air Chief Marshal Dowding (Laurence Oliver), Air Officer Commanding-in-Chief of Fighter Command, making his way to a meeting with a 'Senior Civil Servant' (Harry Andrews). In the background, Olivier recites the text of Dowding's letter imploring the Prime Minister not to send any more Fighter Command squadrons to France, to be squandered away in a battle already lost, making clear the minimum number of squadrons required to defend Britain. This was surely amongst the most significant documents of the twentieth century, and from the film's outset, 'Stuffy' Dowding is upheld, rightly, as a man totally committed to the defence of Britain – bringeth the hour, bringeth the man.

07:47/2:12	We then hop across the Channel and see armour and infantry of the victorious German army (it must be said a somewhat slovenly and scruffy lot of extras from the Spanish army!) entering 'Dunkerque', watched by two elderly and despairing French civilians.
08:16/2:12	Then we see the aftermath of the Dunkirk evacuation, the detritus of war scattered over the beaches and the French port's still-burning oil tanks, seen in the right distance. The evacuation from the beaches, however, occurred at Zuydcoote, Bray Dunes and De Panne, to the north-east of the actual port, so the burning oil tanks should really be to our left. The voiceover comes from Churchill's famous speech, in which he made clear that now France had fallen, 'the Battle of Britain' was about to begin. In history, this is possibly unique, certainly in modern times, that a battle was named before it had even been fought.
08:53/2:12	The film's preamble now over, we have the opening titles to stirring martial music, Generalfeldmarschall Erhard Milch (Dietrich Frauboes), the Luftwaffe's Inspector General, arrives in France to inspect Luftflotte (Air Fleet) 2, commanded by Field Marshal Albert Kesselring (Peter Hager), and in particular the bombers commanded by Oberst Johannes Fink (Wolf Harnisch). Kesselring would be primarily responsible for the forthcoming daylight air assault on England. Fink commanded KG2 'Holzhammer', equipped with Do 17 bombers; the availability of serviceable aircraft for the film, however, dictated the use of Merlin-engined Spanish Air Force CASA 2111s, a design based upon the He 111, which we now see Fink's 'I/KG637' operating. These scenes provide a lasting impression of German aerial might, undefeated to date, and confidence.
13:06/2:12	We then see Milch leaving a conference with Hitler (whom we do not see) in Berlin, in company and conversation with Generalmajor Hans Jeschonnek (Karl-Otto Alberty), the Luftwaffe Chief of Staff. Interestingly,

The Big and 'Fantastic' Story: Battle of Britain in Context 179

General Adolf Galland (left) was the primary German advisor – and on occasions far from easy to deal with. 'Dolfo' is pictured here with Group Captain Douglas Bader at a lecture and book signing in the 1970s – the pair were great friends. (*DSA*)

in this scene, contrary to those previous showing Milch, Kesselring and Fink, Milch observes wryly that the Fuhrer did not consider Britain to be Germany's natural enemy, and that the plan to mount a seaborne invasion of southern England would be a catastrophe. Jeschonnek, conversely, opined that the British were already finished and that such an opportunity would never arise again. This is a short but significant scene, indicating the divided opinion within the German High Command regarding the way forward. A joint service amphibious landing is a vast undertaking, as evidenced by the preparation and resources required for the Allies to successfully return to France on 6 June 1944. The German air force, navy and army was not equipped or trained for such an operation, which was simply not foreseen. Indeed, no-one, least of all Hitler, could have possibly predicted such a lightning advance to the Channel coast and collapse of the old European order. This scene acknowledges that, and also Jeschonnek's over-confidence. Throughout the Battle of Britain, Jeschonnek's staff would provide inaccurate intelligence, leading to poor target selection and a false impression of how the battle was going, the Germans consequently and repeatedly making the wrong strategic and tactical decisions.

13:42/2:12   The viewer is then transported to the British Embassy in Switzerland, for a meeting between the German Foreign Minister, 'Max, Baron von Richter' (Curt Jürgens), a character based upon Joachim von Ribbentropp, straight from a meeting with Hitler, and 'Sir David Kelly, British Ambassador to Switzerland' (Sir Ralph Richardson). Again, the German confidence is emphasised, Von Richter insisting that 'London is ours' and referring to the unsuccessful requests Britain was making to neutral America for direct support – drawing a rousing stiff-upper-lip riposte from Sir David, causing the German to withdraw, offended. The scene concludes with Sir David painfully admitting to his wife, 'Lady Kelly' (Eileen Peel) that 'It's unforgiveable. I lost my temper. The maddening thing is that he's right. We're not ready. We're on our own. We've been playing for time – and its running out!' The scene leaves the viewer in no doubt as to Britain's perilous position – alone – and also pays due acknowledgement, perhaps surprisingly, that behind the scenes, diplomatic negotiations remained ongoing between Britain and Germany to try to reach a peaceful solution – something the British Prime Minister, Winston Churchill, found abhorrent and made this clear in his famous 'fight them on the beaches' speech, which is also referred to. What we learn from this scene is that a diplomatic solution is not an option – and everyone involved knows that sooner, rather than later, the storm will break.

16:49/2:12 We are now transported to an RAF fighter base 'somewhere in England', in June 1940. This is 'Skipper's' squadron, which has exchanged its Hurricanes for Spitfires. It is worth noting that during the actual Battle of Britain, there were two-thirds more Hurricanes than Spitfires, so most Fighter Command squadrons were equipped with the former type. The following year, however, the superior Spitfire, with better all-important high-altitude performance, replaced the Hurricane as the RAF's front-line day fighter, and, after engine and many other upgrades, was ultimately developed through twenty-four marques and remained in production until 1947, and in service until 1954. Some 14,000 Hurricanes were built until the type was discontinued in 1944, whereas 22,000 Spitfires rolled off production lines. Consequently, this is why comparatively few airworthy Hurricanes were available when *Battle of Britain* was made, and why the impression given by the film is that the Spitfire was the RAF's predominant fighter. On the subject of the film's Spitfires, only one, Mk IIA, P7350, had flown in the Battle of Britain, the others being later Merlin-engined marques and even including Griffon-engined types. To the general viewer, none of this detail matters.

17:13/2:12 In this scene, a Spitfire appears, flown by a new pilot, 'Simon' (Nicholas Pennell), who forgets to put his wheels down, and is reminded in the nick of time by a warning flare. The scene implies that Fighter Command was already suffering a severe shortage of pilots, and that operational training was being drastically reduced to ensure a flow of replacements for the squadrons. Certainly, after the Fall of France, during which Fighter Command lost some 300 pilots, and on 1 June 1940, Dowding's operational strength was 1,200 pilots – of which only 906 were combat ready, most of these lacking actual combat experience.

19.13/2:12 Unimpressed with Simon's performance, the unsympathetic Skipper has the youngster airborne again immediately, practising dogfighting and impressing upon him the golden rules of air fighting, 'Before Jerry has you for breakfast'. In truth, after being rested from operations in July 1941, at his own request, Sailor Malan went into training, imparting his wealth of knowledge for the benefit of young pilots such as Simon; it was, in fact, something the great South African ace felt strongly about.

20:40/2:12 Next, we see 'Group Captain Hope' (Nigel Patrick) briefing a group of fighter controllers as to how Fighter Command is organised and how the 'System' works. Again, this is another important scene, providing the viewer clarity as to how Britain will be defended in the battle ahead. Interestingly, one of the 'controllers', is 'Squadron Leader Evans', played by Bill Foxley, an RAF navigator disfigured by burns suffered when his bomber crashed in 1944.

22:00/2:12 Again, we return across the Channel – this time focussing on a fine al fresco coastal dinner with General Theo Osterkamp's (Wilfred von Aacken) fighter pilots, including Majors 'Falke' (Manfred Reddeman) and Föhn (Paul Neuhaus), entertaining Generalfeldmarschall Milch. The cigar-smoking Falke was based upon none other than Adolf Galland, the film's often difficult German technical advisor. An ace and veteran of the Spanish Civil War, during the Battle of Britain Galland was elevated to command JG26, a twelve-squadron-strong fighter group, and went on to succeed his friend Werner Mölders as the fighter pilots' General. Föhn was based upon Mölders, the Kommodore of JG51 and so-called 'Father of Modern Air Fighting', ultimately killed in a flying accident. In this scene exemplifying the total confidence of the Luftwaffe and keenness to 'set about

England', we are also introduced to Falke's brother, 'Hans' (Dagobert Walter) – Galland himself was actually one of four brothers, all fighter pilots, two of which, Wilhem-Ferdinand and Paul, were killed in action.

22:52/2:12   Also in this scene we are introduced to radar, the Inspector General viewing the Chain Home Low Radio Direction Finding (RDF) masts near Dover – just twenty-two miles across the Channel. RDF was a key advantage to the British, providing early warning of German formations assembling over France, and their time, strength and direction of travel towards England. This information was communicated to Fighter Command HQ at Bentley Priory (Stanmore), and thence to the relevant sector airfield operations rooms, which would scramble fighter squadrons accordingly. Whilst in this scene we are introduced to unnamed Stuka aircrew, who will 'deal with' the English's 'secret weapon', the reality is that had Luftwaffe intelligence fully appreciated the crucial significance of RDF, infinitely more effort would have been invested in its destruction.

23:37/2:12   Now we are returned to London, and an informal meeting between Dowding and the 'Minister' (Anthony Nicholls), this being the Liberal Party Leader, Sir Archibald Sinclair, who served as Air Minister in Churchill's coalition war government. The conversation revolves around what was a fortuitous lull between the Fall of France and the Battle of Britain starting, providing the defenders much-needed breathing space to re-group after the continental disaster. The Minister refers to 'Beaverbrook', the Minister for Aircraft Production (whose son, Max, was one of the Few), and his optimism regarding the flow of aircraft from the factories to Dowding's squadrons.

Dowding, however, points out that it is not a lack of aircraft that concerns him – but a potential deficiency in pilots. In terms of fighter aircraft, the two sides were, in fact, fairly evenly matched. Two-thirds of the RAF strength were Hurricanes, however, whereas the majority of enemy

Technical advisor and Battle of Britain Hurricane ace Group Captain Peter Townsend in conversation with Hein Riess – who played a convincing Reichsmarschall Herman Göring. (*DSA*)

fighters were the superior Me 109E – which also had certain technical advantages over the Spitfire too. In terms of aircrew, as the battle progressed, training courses were fore-shortened, but it is important to understand how Fighter Command was deployed. 11 Group, covering

The Big and 'Fantastic' Story: Battle of Britain in Context   185

London and the south-east, was the front-line; 12 Group, defending the industrial Midlands and the North, the second-line. Covering the south-west was 10 Group, and Scotland and Northern Ireland was the responsibility of 13 Group.

Clearly, the hot combat zone was the 11 Group area, but far from concentrating his strength there, Dowding cleverly dispersed squadrons around the country, carefully considering the respective defensive responsibilities of each group. Consequently, after tours of duty in the front line, decimated squadrons were withdrawn to re-build in quieter sectors, before relieving a similarly depleted unit and returning to the front line. By shepherding resources in this way, there would never be a shortage of aircraft, pilots or operational squadrons in the battle ahead. Fighter Command casualties were certainly critical by the first week of September 1940, but never dropped to an unmanageable level. For this, Dowding deserves great credit – but the facts, of course, do not provide the myth-making film-maker much ammunition.

25:16/2:12   Now we leave Whitehall's corridors of power and return to a fighter squadron in southern England. In this scene, we also see how equally keen RAF fighter pilots were to engage the enemy, with 'Pilot Officer Charlie Lambert' (Alan Tucker) requesting permission from Squadron Leader Canfield (Michael Caine) for 'an instrument check', and hurrying off to get airborne.

25:29/2:12   We see Harvey promoted to squadron leader, complete with 'Canada' shoulder-flash, having handed over command of '188 Squadron', also now Spitfire-equipped, to Squadron Leader Canfield, leaving for a new posting in Scotland. 'Sergeant-Pilot Chris' (David Griffin) requests permission for a test flight, but, wiser now after some advice from Harvey, Canfield refuses this.

26:37/2:12   Squadron Leader Harvey arrives at and parks his green MG outside 'The Jackdaw' (at Denton, near the Kent Battle of Britain Museum at Hawkinge, both essential locations for the enthusiast to visit). We are now given a glimpse of the difficulties experienced by wartime marriages, and some male attitudes towards women serving. Inside the quintessential English pub, 'Section Officer Maggie Harvey' (Susannah York) of the WAAF, patiently awaits her fighter pilot husband's arrival. Unfortunately, a domestic soon brews, when Maggie, who, we later discover, is serving at a busy southern fighter station, is reluctant to comply with her husband's insistence that she should apply for a posting and join him in Scotland. Unable to talk his wife around, exit Harvey, just as Local Defence Volunteers (Home Guard), armed with shotguns and pitchforks, finish their drill in the car park, leaving behind his watery-eyed and beautiful wife (complete with 1960s hair-do).

28:53/2:12 Back at Canfield's airfield, Charlie is overdue, causing grave concern. Suddenly, a Hurricane, 'out of juice very likely', lands unexpectedly – the pilots at dispersal disconcerted to see that the pilot is their Air Officer Commanding (AOC), Air Vice-Marshal Keith Park (Trevor Howard). Interestingly, as the AOC enters the dispersal hut, we see displayed on the wall next to the Orderly Clerk Sailor Malan's famous 'Ten Rules of Air Fighting' – which was not published, in fact, until 1942. In this turn of events, however, we learn that this is a coastal airfield and of the AOC's concern about losing pilots unnecessarily over the Channel. Unfortunately, Lambert had flown over the sea, looking for trouble – and found it: he was ambushed, out of the sun, by Major Falke, and shot down. Baling out into the water, Lambert was not rescued – and at this stage RAF Air Sea Rescue, unlike the German set-up, was as embryonic as it was ad hoc.

31:12/2:12 We now return across the Channel to see the cocky and arrogant Falke preparing to celebrate his latest aerial victory by having dinner in Boulogne with his friend Föhn, who, whilst awaiting Falk, is entertained by Hans and other officers. Again, the Germans' high-morale and total confidence is emphasised. The revelry is cut short, however, when both Kommodoren are urgently called to a conference at Osterkamp's Wissant HQ. En-route, the officers are held up by a great column of barges being moved by road to Calais and Boulogne in preparation for Operation Seelöwe

The Big and 'Fantastic' Story: Battle of Britain in Context   187

– the seaborne invasion of England. The impression given is that German preparations and resources for this colossal undertaking were up to the challenge – in reality they were not, although barges were converted and assembled in the Channel ports for this purpose.

34:02/2:12   We now jump to 'Eagle Day', which, the caption tells us, was 10 August 1940. It was not. Although originally planned for that day, bad weather delayed this major attack until three days later. This, however, loses a whole month of the Battle of Britain. So far as the British were later concerned, the start date was 10 July 1940, this opening phase featuring the Luftwaffe cautiously probing coastal defences, and especially attacking shipping in the Channel. Apart from the isolated loss of Pilot Officer Lambert on a test flight, this period, the 'Kanal Kampf' (Channel battle) is ignored by the film-makers. This is a pity, notwithstanding that in any case the fighting actually began on 4 July 1940, because this ignores the loss of life suffered by Fighter Command and merchant seamen. Nonetheless, we do know that on 10 August 1940, Dowding had at his disposal 1,100 serviceable fighters – but only 750 combat ready pilots. Returning to 'Eagle Day', we see Fink briefing his bomber crews, using a pointer to indicate target airfields – although where his stick lands on the map bears no semblance to the reality of these geographic locations.

34:30/2:12   In the briefings on their respective fighter airfields, Falke and Föhn emphasise the importance of height – and the need to carefully monitor and conserve fuel. Like the British fighters, the Me 109, which Merlin-engined Spanish Air Force Hispano-Buchons masqueraded as in the film, was designed as a short-range defensive interceptor – not a long-range escort or offensive fighter. What the German fighter pilots were now being asked to do, escorting bombers to a distant strategic target, was contrary to the designer's intention – more of which later. The Germans would also have to make two sea-crossings per sortie on a single-engine – a nervous undertaking for any pilot at the best of times

188   Battle of Britain: The Movie

– hence the emphasis on fuel states. Indeed, the 109s only had sufficient fuel for twenty minutes of combat flying over south-east England.

36:58/2:12   The subsequent aerial combat sequence features Stukas dive-bombing, with a degree of success, radar installations at Ventnor on the Isle of Wight, and Dover. Interestingly, the young WAAF radar operator at Ventnor ('I'm afraid the raid is entering my ground-range, Stanmore') is a twenty-two-year-old Dame Maureen Lipman. The Stukas are intercepted by Canfield's Spitfires – 'Pinetree Squadron'. Over the white cliffs of Sussex's iconic Seven Sisters and Beachy Head, the Spitfires pounce – although with formation and other flying best-suited to camera angles than the Fighter Command Book of Tactics. The unescorted and hapless dive-bombers are soon knocked about, however, indicating the Stukas vulnerability, the type suffering such heavy losses that it was withdrawn from the actual battle. In

Advertisement for Dinky's die-cast Spitfire Mk II associated with the film. (*DSA*)

The Big and 'Fantastic' Story: Battle of Britain in Context   189

this scene, German aircraft hit invariably burst into flame and blew up – which many of the Few confirmed to me never happened in their actual experience.

42:43/2:12   We then see the 'He 111s' escorted by 'Me 109s', their formations' course plotted from the ground by the Observer Corps (OC). Once the enemy had crossed the coast, RDF at this time was of no use – hence the importance of the OC, which is not emphasised sufficiently.

43:07/2:12   The information from radar and the OC having been received by Fighter Command HQ Operations Room and 'filtered' out to the relevant Sector Airfield Operations Room, the Clerk, 'LAC Arnold' (David McKail), answers the telephone at Squadron Leader Skipper's 'Rabbit Squadron' dispersal: Arnold's cry of 'Two Section: *SCRAMBLE!*' sets the pilots running for their Spitfires, which take-off just as the 'Look-out' sounds the hand-cranked air-raid siren – which the complacent station personnel assume to be a practice. Fighter squadrons were actually divided into two flights of six machines each, 'A' and 'B', which were sub-divided into two sections of three. Each section was colour-coded, and each pilot in every section numbered one to three (hence, for example, Blue 2, Red 1 etc). Correctly, then, Arnold should have shouted for whatever flight or colour-coded section was on immediate readiness.

44:21/2:12   Now, we have a glimpse of wider life on the same RAF fighter airfield, the Station Commander, 'Group Captain Baker' (Kenneth More) rebuking 'Warrant Officer Warwick' (Michael Bates) for there being 'muck and filth everywhere', standards having slipped, apparently, on account of long hours being worked. Section Officer Maggie Harvey is also in Baker's sights on account of some WAAFs having been noted using the 'men's trenches' during air raid practice – an indication of how the sexes were segregated at the time. The 'Groupie' also complains that WAAFs are using gas mask cases as handbags – all very petty – when bombs start exploding across the airfield, and Group Captain Baker rushes to the nearest slit trench – which, ironically, is a female shelter...

46.38/2:12 The confused Arnold then takes another call: a Squadron scramble. Squadron Leader Skipper, having only just landed is unimpressed and demands to speak to the 'Duty Controller' – just as bombs start exploding on the airfield and, there being no further doubt, sending Skipper and his remaining pilots sprinting for their aircraft. The still bewildered Simon is unsure what to do, as Skipper barks 'Don't just stand there – get one up!' Without delay, with bombs exploding all around, the Spitfires are off – although at least one is destroyed whilst taxying. This happened. On 31 August 1940, 11 Group's sector airfields were being truly hammered, the Spitfires of 54 Squadron scrambling during a heavy raid on Hornchurch; eight Spitfires scrambled safely whilst one section of three were completely wrecked by exploding bombs whilst taking off – although miraculously all three pilots, including the tough Kiwi ace Flight Lieutenant Al Deere, survived.

48:44/2:12 Rabbit Squadron assembles in the air, the bad-tempered Skipper taking issue with the tardy ground controller, and the inexperienced Simon's poor formation flying. Inevitably, the high-flying 109s bounce and kill the bewildered 'Red 2' in their usual high-speed diving pass.

50:32/2:12 Back at Group Captain Baker's airfield, the damage is extensive. Section Officer Harvey is stunned by a line of dead, blanket-covered WAAFs. Shocked, the young officer goes to light a cigarette when the experienced and professional airman Warwick cannot believe his eyes, shouting, regardless of rank 'Put that cigarette out! The mains have gone! Can't you smell gas?!' In that superb moment of highly emotional cinema, Warwick becomes the focus of all Maggie's fear and rage: 'Don't you yell at me, Mr Warwick!' In that instance she snaps out of her shell-shocked state and gets on with it. It is a great and fondly remembered scene – but, in reality, just three WAAFs lost their lives during the actual Battle of Britain: one died of injuries sustained when Detling was bombed, another at Biggin Hill, and the last, who was pregnant, was tragically killed whilst off-duty and shielding her mother-in-law from shrapnel during a raid on Eastbourne, where the pair were enjoying a shopping trip. Nonetheless, the scene gets the point across, that 'they' also served – and, of course, a number of WAAFs were decorated for their bravery during the battle.

52:31/2:12 As the raid withdraws, we now join Air Vice-Marshal Park in his 11 Group underground Operations Room at Uxbridge (now open to the public, the 'Battle of Britain Bunker'), as two controllers, 'Wing Commander Willoughby' (Robert Flemyng) and his assistant (Tom Chatto) lament damage to the airfields and suggest that the fighter squadrons should be moved North of the Thames – which Park is rightly having none of.

52:52/2:12 We now see Group Captain Baker surveying the colossal damage to his airfield, this scene leaving us in no doubt as to how badly the airfields were damaged and disrupted, with even some sector operations rooms having to be set up in civilian properties off the station.

53:51/2:12 The next scene shows Jeschonnek providing intelligence for a major raid being planned on north-east England, by bombers based in Norway. 'Even a Spitfire', he gloats, 'can't be in two places at once'. This tells us two things: firstly, that the Germans failed to understand how Dowding rotated his squadrons around the Command, and maintained sufficient fighters in all sectors to meet their geographic defensive responsibilities; and secondly that the Spitfire was an especially respected opponent.

55:40/2:12 Squadron Leader Harvey's northern-based Spitfires subsequently intercept the unescorted 'Heinkels', which immediately break formation upon being attacked. This would not happen. German bomber tactics relied upon carefully practised and rehearsed formations providing mutual protection. To break formation was suicide – leaving the individual aircraft wide-open to attack – but it made

192   Battle of Britain: The Movie

Two 'film' books published by Purnell in 1969. (*DSA*)

Air Chief Marshal Sir Christopher Foxley-Norris, Chairman of the Battle of Britain Fighter Association (extreme left), with composer Ron Goodwin (second left) at the launch of the original "Battle of Britain: The Movie", Worcester Guildhall, May 2000.

The Big and 'Fantastic' Story: Battle of Britain in Context 193

for good cinema. The actual attack, on 15 August 1940, was made by seventy-two He 111s escorted by twenty-one twin-engined Me 110s, and met by various squadrons of Spitfires and Hurricanes It was a disastrous day for Luftflotte 5, which lost a total of eighty-one aircrew, and indicated the folly of sending bombers to England unprotected by the Me 109. These are, however, terrific aerial combat sequences – set to Ron Goodwin's rousing *Battle of Britain Theme* score.

58:57/2:12 Back at base, Harvey's pilots make out their combat reports to the Intelligence Officer (Basil Dignam), and 'Peter' (Myles Hoyle) is disappointed to learn that the He 111 he has destroyed has to be shared with two other pilots, who also attacked the same enemy aircraft, as so often happened.

59:33/2:12 Squadron Leader Harvey, however, takes issue with Peter for victory-rolling over 'his' airfield before landing. To be fair, Harvey had a point: on 10 April 1941, Pilot Officer Peter Chesters of 74 Squadron destroyed an Me 109 over Kent, then jubilantly victory-rolled over Manston airfield, badly misjudging things and crashing into the parade ground – killing himself.

1:00/2:12 We then switch to Fighter Command HQ, Bentley Priory, and a staff officer (John Savident) excitedly sharing with a colleague (John Tatham) the claim figures arising from the northern raid, keen to share these with 'Stuffy' Dowding. Whilst pleased, Dowding voices more concerns over pilot shortages to his Senior Air Staff Officer (SASO), Air Vice-Marshal Evill (Michael Redgrave), although in fact Fighter Command had by now been reinforced by pilots from other commands and the Fleet Air Arm – but these men had to be converted to modern fighters and lacked combat experience. And therein lies the rub: Dowding's concern was not the overall number of pilots but the number of experienced pilots being lost. By this time, in fact, Fighter Command's establishment had risen from 1,482 in June 1940, to 1,558 by 17 August 1940, of which 1,379 were operational – how many were combat ready at that time is unrecorded, but we do know that the figure had dropped from 906 on 1 June

1940 to 735 by 1 September, and on 1 November 1940 – the day after the Battle of Britain officially ended – this reached an all-time low of 673. In the scene, Dowding rejects a proposal to make the new Polish and Czechoslovak squadrons operational on the grounds that they could still not understand English sufficiently well to be anything other than a 'menace to themselves and everyone else' in the air.

By this stage of the battle, however, this is not strictly true – there were already a number of Polish and Czech pilots serving in RAF squadrons (alongside men from Britain, the Commonwealth, and those from other occupied lands, including French and Belgians – not to mention a small number of volunteers from neutral America). On 10 July 1940, the Czech 310 Squadron was formed at Duxford, and 302 (Polish) at Leconfield, both in 12 Group. On 29 July 1940, the Czechs were made operational, and were a component part of the 12 Group 'Big Wing', led by Squadron Leader Bader and based at Duxford (of which more later). By 15 August 1940, 302 Squadron was also declared operational, becoming the first Polish squadron to be so, this unit also subsequently participating in 12 Group Wing operations.

The second Polish squadron, 303, however, was not formed until 2 August 1940 – and this unit was not operational by mid-August, when the scene in question is supposed to have taken place. These new squadrons of foreign nationals had British squadron and flight commanders, to ease their passage into RAF operational and other procedures, who were shadowed by their Polish and Czech counterparts, and everything was being done, in fact, to resolve the language issue and get them into the line. At Duxford, for example, the Station Commander, Group Captain A.B. 'Woody' Woodhall garnered help from the BBC, which cut an LP record for him translating aerial commands in English into Polish and Czech. Indeed, it was to everyone's benefit to get the Poles in particular into action, as some of their number had experienced combat over their homeland, and in France. This scene therefore, does neither Dowding or Fighter Command justice, simply helping fuel a myth (as we will see).

1:01/2:12   We then see a major raid developing in the Fighter Command Operations Room. Skipper's Rabbit Squadron,

The Big and 'Fantastic' Story: Battle of Britain in Context 195

already airborne, intercepts a formation of bombers – but the Spitfires are bounced from above by a large force of Me 109s. The following action is superb, and these aerial scenes are the film's real tour de force. Off Eastbourne (a modern high-rise building in which is clearly visible), Sergeant-Pilot Andy is shot down and takes to his parachute. Interestingly, and purely as an aside, in a number of combat sequences we, the viewer, are placed in a Spitfire cockpit – only to actually be peering out of a Hurricane's windscreen…

1:05/2:12 Back at base, Skipper pays full acknowledgement to the Squadron's groundcrews, working tirelessly to keep the Spitfires flying. Sergeant-Pilot Andy's reappearance after being rescued from the Channel provokes rebuke for getting bounced – followed by the Skipper adopting a more paternalistic attitude and giving the cold and wet sergeant a lift back to his accommodation.

1:07/2:12 We are next exposed to Canfield's anger and frustration at his airfield having been wrecked by German bombs, and dissatisfaction at being dispersed to operate from a former civilian flying club. All sector stations had satellite airfields, some of which had primitive facilities and only tented accommodation, such as Fowlmere, Duxford's satellite. Others, such as Gravesend, for example, had previously been civilian airfields. Cranfield makes an acerbic observation that unless 'someone' protects the airfields whilst 11 Group's fighters are airborne, the destruction will continue.

1:08/2:12 At Canfield's new airfield, he and 'Pinetree Squadron' are at cockpit readiness, propellers turning: 'How much longer, Ops? The engine's overheating and so am I. We either stand-down or blow up. Which do you want?'. Then up goes a flare and the Spitfires scramble.

1:09/2:12 In the next sequence we see Air Vice-Marshal Park, a man under pressure if ever there was one, considering the battering his airfields were getting, insists that the controller reminds 12 Group fighters that their task is essential: to protect 11 Group's airfields whilst his fighters are engaged further forward. In reality, by this time, a row had broken out over 12 Group's apparent inability to effectively provide the cover required and as demanded by the System. On 15 August 1940, for example, 12 Group's Fowlmere-based 19 Squadron's Spitfires arrived too late over Martlesham Heath to prevent it being badly damaged. 12 Group, commanded by Air Vice-Marshal Trafford Leigh-Mallory, however, argued that it was being requested too late to have any realistic chance of intercepting the enemy, and also accused 11 Group of 'hogging' the battle. The problem was the limitations of RDF in use at that time, the comparatively limited warning time it gave offset against the speed of the aircraft involved, both in terms of those attacking and defending. 11 Group, however, was fighting the battle exactly as per Dowding's wishes, intercepting the enemy using small, flexible, formations, in order to carefully preserve resources. That said, Park was not averse to using wings of two or more squadrons when the occasion demanded, and would soon use Spitfire squadrons in pairs as a high-flying protective umbrella.

1:10/2:12 In the ensuing action, Pinetree Squadron is bounced by 109s (another superb aerial combat scene) and Canfield is killed: 'He just … Blew up!', and an airfield operations room is bomb-damaged, indicating that the Germans reached their target.

1:14/2:12 A furious Air Vice-Marshal Park is then seen having flown to a meeting with Dowding, bitterly complaining to a Fighter Command staff officer, a group captain (Jack Gwillim) that 'God knows how many aircraft we'll have in the morning – all because 12 Group didn't do their stuff. Leigh-Mallory's so-called "Big Wings" might as well stay on the ground for all the good they are'. This leads perfectly into the next scene, which in many ways is a significant one.

1:14.27/2:12 We now join Air Vice-Marshal Park and Air Vice-Marshal Leigh-Mallory (Patrick Wymark) at a meeting with Air Chief Marshal Dowding's office at Fighter Command HQ, Bentley Priory. This room has, in fact, ben preserved as part of the excellent Bentley Priory Museum, and can be visited. In this meeting, the two group commanders argue about the effectiveness or otherwise of Leigh-Mallory's

The Big and 'Fantastic' Story: Battle of Britain in Context

'Big Wing'. This requires explanation. Amongst Leigh-Mallory's squadron commanders was the swashbuckling, legless dynamo Douglas Bader, who was unable to tolerate playing a secondary role in 12 Group and not being at the sharp end. Bader was continually exasperated that 11 Group did not call for (or need!) his help. On 30 August 1940 (again, of which more later), 11 Group did request 12 Group's assistance, and Bader's 242 Squadron caught its first sight of a mass German raid, which it intercepted over Hatfield, with some success.

A euphoric Bader reported that had he more fighters at his disposal, greater damage to the enemy could have been effected, and that, contrary to the System and Dowding's well-thought out strategy, which balanced conserving resources against the needs of defending targets before they were bombed, whilst achieving the greatest enemy losses, several 12 Group squadrons should operate together, as a 'wing', under his overall leadership, heading straight for the action or patrolling over the combat area in readiness for an attack.

The concept was flawed from the outset, however. In their excitement, Bader's pilots had failed to notice that 11 Group squadrons, amongst them the highly experienced Nos 1 and 222, were also engaged and recorded successes. Indeed, we now know that 242 Squadron overclaimed that day by at least 4:1, so the results were actually nothing like as successful as they first appeared. Both the ambitious Leigh-Mallory, and Duxford's Station Commander and Sector Controller, Group Captain Woodhall, agreed with Bader. It was decided that 242 would fly with 310 Squadron, both from Duxford, whilst the Fowlmere-based Spitfires of 19 Squadron provided top cover. Bader first led the Wing into action on 7 September 1940, claiming more successes, and so it went on – the overclaiming ratio reaching an all-time high of 7:1. These figures, however, were accepted and two more squadrons were added to the 'Big Wing'.

There was a long history of hostility on Leigh-Mallory's behalf towards both Dowding, who he had vowed to see 'replaced', and Park, of whom he was jealous, and, supported by the Deputy Chief of the Air Staff, Air Vice-Marshal Sholto Douglas, the 12 Group commander initiated a 'dirty little intrigue', involving even Churchill himself, arguing that mass fighter formations should be adopted as standard, and that the tactics employed by Dowding and Park were comparatively ineffective. We know today, from rigorous analysis, that 11 Group's claims were infinitely more accurate that 12's, and that the Big Wing concept simply did not, and could not, work. Because the claims were accepted with little question, however, there was a very different impression at the time. Ultimately, Dowding and Park were called to a meeting at the Air Ministry in October 1940, at which, to their surprise, they were called upon by the Air Staff to justify their tactics, and at which the Big Wing protagonists advanced support of their theory.

Cutting a very long story short, there is little doubt that this controversy led to the replacement of Dowding and Park by Douglas and Leigh-Mallory respectively, almost immediately after the Battle of Britain had been won. Both men remained bitter about their treatment, and were concerned at how both they and the controversy would be treated by the film. Returning to the actual scene, the main point is that it never happened. Dowding was a hands-off Commander-in-Chief, who set out his instructions and left his group commanders to carry them out. Indeed, he was not a politician and only realised the danger from the Big Wing camp too late.

After the war, he admitted that not having intervened in the dispute between Leigh-Mallory and Park was his one big command failing. Indeed, at no time during the Battle of Britain did Dowding call his group commanders together for conference; had he done so after the issue over Martlesham on 15 August 1940, the Big Wing Controversy may have been avoided. In the event, Lord Dowding and Air Chief Marshal Sir Keith Park, as they had become, were sympathetically treated by *Battle of Britain*, which, unlike *Reach for the Sky*, indicated antipathy over tactics between the two group commanders behind the scenes. When Lord Dowding visited the film set at Pinewood Studios, it was none other than Group Captain Sir Douglas Bader who insisted on pushing the old man's wheelchair – who Dowding actually held responsible for 'much of the trouble'.

1:15/2:12   Leaving behind arguments over 'Big Wings' and 'Small Wings', we move to London's Savoy Hotel and a bedroom scene with Colin and Maggie Harvey – which again draws into the big story issues besetting wartime marriages. The night, however, is shattered by German bombs exploding

The Big and 'Fantastic' Story: Battle of Britain in Context 199

– this being the first time the capital was bombed, on 24 August 1940, an accidental occurrence as Hitler had placed London off limits whilst still reluctant to commit to an all-out air offensive against the British civilian population. Churchill, however, immediately ordered a retaliatory raid on Berlin the following night, made by eighty-one Wellingtons and Hampdens, although only half found and bombed the cloud-obscured target, causing the death of just one elephant at the city's zoo. The bombing of Berlin in the film, however, indicates the peacetime atmosphere and lack of air raid precautions, a direct contrast to the blackout of British cities – another indication of German over-confidence.

1:22/2:12 RAF Bomber Command's raid on Berlin incensed Hitler, who we see in the film (Rolf Stiefel) addressing the Bund Deutscher Mädel (BDM), the League of German Girls, and promising to flatten British cities in retribution. This was a turning point in the Battle of Britain – because Hitler now ordered a turn away from the bombing of airfields, which was actually increasingly successful, and instead prioritised the destruction of London.

1:24/2:12 Frustrated at his Luftwaffe's inability to achieve the required decision over England, and with new orders from Hitler, we see Reichsmarschall Herman Göring (Hein Reiss), the Luftwaffe chief himself, arriving by special train in the 'Pas-de-Calais' – a most unlikely looking Pas-de-Calais, which is essentially a flat landscape, it must be said, the Spanish station used for the scene overlooked by a mountain. The Reichsmarschall is met by a reception committee of senior officers, including Kesselring and Osterkamp.

By now, the majority of Me 109 fighters had been moved into the Pas-de-Calais, ready to escort bombers to a new target: London. This was not, however, just because of the Berlin attack. To achieve aerial supremacy, the Germans needed to destroy Fighter Command. So far, however, thanks to the way Dowding had organised his Command and rotated squadrons, the Luftwaffe had failed to lure the defending fighters into the air for destruction en masse. London, however, was believed to be the one target that Dowding would commit his force in its entirety to defend.

1:26/2:12   The arrogant Göring and his staff are seen on the French cliffs at Cap-Gris-Nez, gleefully watching a huge aerial armada making its way overhead towards the British capital. This did happen: on 7 September 1940.

1:27/2:12   At a sector operations room in south-east England, the Controller (Eric Dodson) vectors Skipper's Rabbit Squadron in anticipation of another airfield raid – only for the vexed Skipper to find no enemy aircraft in sight. Meanwhile, the confused Controller telephones 11 Group HQ at Uxbridge – where it is realised that whilst squadrons are up over airfields, the Germans have stolen a march and are heading for the undefended city of London.

1.28/2:12   On the ground, East End 'mud larks' watch the approaching phalanx of German aircraft, disputing whether they be 'Messerschmitts' or ''einkels'. This is the first big attack on the capital, starting on 7 September 1940, which went on around-the-clock, the German bombers flying a shuttle service back and forth, guided to the burning docklands like moths to a flame.

1:32/2:12   On the ground, amidst the bombs that night we again meet Sergeant-Pilot Andy, on leave after having baled out into the Channel, and seeking his family – which his wife (Isla Sinclair, also complete with 1960s hair-do) has brought back to London from safety in the country. Andy finds his wife and two young boys in a 'Rest Centre', but answers the call for volunteers to help rescue a family in 'Shaw Street'. The devastation to the East End slums is apparent, the bombed family found dead – and upon return, Andy is devastated to find the Rest Centre destroyed and his family killed. These scenes emphasise the civilian loss of life, and that the East Enders suffered – and that servicemen also had to deal with personal tragedy.

1:35/2:12   Staying with Sergeant-Pilot Andy, we see him lodging with Squadron Leader Skipper and his family and preparing to leave the house to go on readiness at the airfield. Considering the segregation of ranks on the ground at the time, NCOs and officers each in their respective messes or sharing accommodation with men of at least equal rank and status,

The Big and 'Fantastic' Story: Battle of Britain in Context 201

	this is a highly improbable scenario. As the pair leave the house, we see a 1960s doorbell – which enthusiasts delight in pointing out to this day!
1:37/2:12	We now come to some real myth-making – as Air Vice-Marshal Park, watching the progress of a raid in his Uxbridge Bunker, is told that plot 'T5' is 'A training squadron … the Poles', leading the Duty Controller, Wing Commander Willoughby (Robert Flemyng) to order 'Get them out of it, get them down'. This implies that this particular unit is the only Polish squadron, which, as previously explained, was not the case, and other Polish pilots were operational and serving in RAF squadrons. This order is communicated by radio to 'Blackhawk Leader', the Hurricane-equipped unit's English CO, 'Squadron Leader Edwards' (Barry Foster). This character is based upon Squadron Leader Ronald Gustave Kellett, a pre-war auxiliary who formed 303 (Polish) Squadron at Northolt on 2 August 1940. On 30 August 1940, 303 Squadron was up from Northolt on an affiliation exercise with Blenheim bombers, when the raid came in against Hatfield, intercepted by Bader's 242 Squadron and 11 Group units. In the film, Blackhawk Leader gives his pilots a course to steer, away from the trouble, but one, 'Ox' (Andrezej Scibor) sights the enemy, leading to excited Polish chatter over the ether.

Unable to contain himself, Ox responds 'Repeat please', feigning receipt of or ignorance of the order, and peels off to engage the Germans – followed, one by one, by his comrades, whilst Squadron Leader Edwards flies on, momentarily, oblivious, until out of the corner of his eye he catches sight of what is going on and with a cry of 'Oh, Gawd, streuth!' and makes after his errant Poles, by now successfully in action.

This is what really happened. In 1978, Wing Commander Kellett recalled that 'On the last training occasion we had twelve Blenheims as "targets" when we were warned that enemy aircraft were in the vicinity. We were to guard the bombers. I ordered the Squadron to assemble above and behind the bombers and cease "attacking". It was, however, too much for Paskiewicz, who, having seen an enemy aircraft, attacked and shot it down. Fortunately, the Blenheims were not attacked, and I reported to

Group Captain Vincent (Northolt's Station Commander) and Air Vice-Marshal Park, that we were ready for combat'.

Flying Officer Ludwik Paskiewicz (Green 1) reported that: 'We took off in two flights (A and B) for exercises in attacking Blenheims, at 1615 hrs. After climbing to 10,000 feet, we flew northward. After a while we noticed ahead a number of aircraft carrying out various evolutions. The centre of the commotion seemed to be about 1,000 feet below us, to starboard. I reported it to the CO, Squadron Leader Kellett, by Radio Telephone, and, as he did not seem to reply, I opened up the throttle and went in the direction of the enemy. I saw the rest of the Flight some 300 yards behind me; behind me were the burning suburbs of some town and a Hurricane diving with smoke trailing behind it. Then I noticed, at my own altitude, a bomber with twin rudders – probably a Dornier – turning in my direction. When he noticed me, he dived sharply. I turned over and dived after him. When turning over I noticed the black crosses on the wings. Then I aimed at the fuselage and opened fire. When I drew very close, I pressed down for a new attack and then I saw another Hurricane attacking and a German baling out by parachute. The Dorner went into a steep turn, and then I gave him another burst. He dived and then hit the ground and burst into flames. I then approached the other Hurricane and saw its markings: VC I. I have been firing at an enemy aircraft for the first time in my life.'

Paskiewicz was credited with a 'Do 17' destroyed near St Albans, shared with Pilot Officer JB Wicks of 56 Squadron. The enemy aircraft concerned was actually a Me 110 of 4/ZG76, however, the starboard engine of which was disabled by Paskiewicz before being attacked by Wicks and exploding at Barley Beans Farm, Kimperton.

According to *Destiny Can Wait: The History of the Polish Air Force in Great Britain* (1949), 'Squadron Leader Kellett neither restrained Paskiewicz nor allowed the other pilots to follow him. He continued the exercise, which consisted then of protecting, instead of "attacking", the Blenheims'. Wing Commander Johnny Kent, Kellett's 'A' Flight Commander, wrote in his memoir, *One of the Few*, that over this first victory, 'the Poles were absolutely cock-a-hoop over it. Ronald Kellett was so pleased with the way they had behaved that he immediately asked permission to declare the Squadron "operational".'

Certainly, all of Kellett's pilots but one had obeyed his order, and there was clearly sympathy for Paskiewicz's ill-discipline. Nonetheless, what could have happened to the Blenheims, had all the Poles followed

Paskiewicz, as in the film, leaving them unprotected, is not difficult to imagine.

It is not widely appreciated that certain aircraft within a squadron at this time were fitted with a navigational device called 'Pip Squeak', which automatically blocked all transmissions for fourteen seconds of every minute whilst broadcasting a 'fix' on the aircraft's location. It is likely that a squadron commander's aircraft would be fitted with this device, which may explain Squadron Leader Kellett's lack of response to Paskiewicz. Either way, the actual circumstances involving 303 Squadron on 30 August 1940, were very different to the exaggerated but entertaining version in *Battle of Britain*.

> 1:39/2:12 In the next scene, we have an initially angry Squadron Leader Edwards delivering his Polish pilots a rocket via a translator, 'Pasco' (Mark Malicz), for their indiscipline, concluding with the good news that the Squadron is 'operational'. Then, Park and Dowding discuss the development, Dowding stating that he was 'wrong about the Poles', and Park pointing out that there was a second Polish squadron, which Dowding then agreed to likewise make operational, along with the Czechs and Canadians.

As we have seen, the other Polish unit, 302, was already operational, and had scored its first victory on 20 August 1940 – ten days before 303 Squadron. The Czechs of 310 Squadron, operational since 29 July 1940, would make their first kill the day after 303. Similarly, the Canadians of No 1 Squadron RCAF were also already operational, and scored their first victory against the Luftwaffe on 26 August 1940. These facts, therefore, again tell a different story to the film – which presents an exaggerated incident involving 303 Squadron, and that Squadron's success, as sole catalyst for the other foreign squadrons also being made operational. Clearly this is not true.

The reader may wonder why this point is being laboured? This is because, without detracting in any way from the Squadron's achievements and courage, in recent years a substantial cult has built up around 303, not least inspired by *Battle of Britain* – and the historian must always strive to accurately contextualise things. To my mind, upholding 303 Squadron as the film-makers did in Battle of Britain was disrespectful to the achievements of the existing foreign squadrons – all three of which were already fully operational by the time of Paskiewicz's unauthorised combat over St Albans. This is one example of the actual story being even more dramatic than the cinematic version – if only it had been possible to somehow show in the limited time available.

1:40/2:12   Dowding and Park then step out onto the terrace of Bentley Priory, watching the night-bombing of London, the former commenting that there was 'nothing we can do about it'. Unfortunately, this was largely true: Britain's night defences remained in their infancy, hence why the Germans shifted their main bombing effort to the hours of darkness. Although less accurate than daylight bombing, the trade-off for the enemy was that nocturnal operations were safer, at least at that time, before the advent of Airborne Interception radar equipped and dedicated night-fighting aircraft arrived. In this scene, Park makes the point that the Germans' change of tack is permitting his airfields to recover – and Dowding remarks that if the enemy concentrates on London the Luftwaffe has further to travel to the target and back – allowing more RAF fighters to be brought into action, including 12 Group and Leigh-Malory's 'Big Wing'. This was all certainly the case.

1:42/2:12   We now approach the fighting's climax, with the Germans still targeting London. Echoing Dowding's prophecy, we watch various RAF squadrons being vectored to intercept the enemy, including the arrival of 'a friendly wing' – greeted by one Hurricane pilot with 'Bloody marvellous'. It has traditionally been written that the arrival over London on Battle of Britain Day, 15 September 1940, of Douglas Bader at the head of five 12 Group squadrons was a crushing blow to enemy morale. Having researched the 'Big Wing' in minute detail for many years, this author has found no specific evidence from the Luftwaffe side to support that claim. German aircrew certainly were demoralised by the overall numbers of RAF fighters in action that day, but nowhere is it recorded that this was caused specifically by the Big Wing's arrival. What Bader's appearance did

The Big and 'Fantastic' Story: Battle of Britain in Context 205

	undoubtedly do, however, was massively inspire and uplift the morale of 11 Group's outnumbered pilots that day – and this comment in the film acknowledges that. What is confusing, however, is that in these incredible scenes of fighter versus fighter combat, Canfield's voice is identifiable – who is supposedly already killed in action – and Harvey's, who is still in Scotland!
1:44/2:12	What follows are absolutely superb scenes of aerial combat, and we hear Harvey's voice giving commands to his pilots. We see the Pole, 'Ox', shot down, baling out and amusingly mistaken for a German upon landing by a farmer (John Baskcomb).
1:47/2:12	With so many RAF fighters, the Germans are roughly handled, a badly damaged He 111 struggling back to France, trailing smoke and flying low over German troops, giving them cause for concern regarding how the air assault on England was going, before crash-landing with badly wounded crewmen aboard. Clearly, the tide of battle has turned in the defenders' favour.
1:48/2:12	This turn of events, however, leads to a furious Göring berating his high and field commanders. Those assembled explain that the aircrew and their machines are tired, after weeks of fighting, and that the enemy is now attacking in greater strength. To a degree, this was true, the Big Wing by now, with political support, being virtually a law unto itself, roaming over London and Kent, although its impact was actually negligible. Göring rants that the fighter pilots are cowards and should be escorting the bombers more closely – ordering that this will from now on be the case – drawing fire from the fighter leader who argues that this deprives his pilots of the advantage of surprise. Then Göring calms down and offers help, asking what his commanders need. Falke's response was 'A squadron of Spitfires!'

This informal conference did indeed take place, as General Galland remembered: 'We received many more harsh words. Finally, as his time ran short, he grew more amiable and asked what were the requirements for our squadrons? "I should like an outfit of Spitfires for my Group".

After blurting this out, I had rather a shock, because it was not really meant that way. Of course, fundamentally I preferred our Me 109 to the Spitfire, but I was unbelievably vexed at the lack of understanding and the stubbornness with which the command gave us orders we could not execute – or only incompletely – as a result of many of the shortcomings for which we were not to blame. Such brazen-faced impudence made even Göring speechless. He stomped off, growling as he went'.

1:49/2:12   We then return to the air and another great raid on London. In this sequence, Pilot Officer Archie (Edward Fox) attacks a He 111 but is shot-up by the rear-gunner; wheeling around, although trailing smoke, the Spitfire pilot returns to the attack, shooting down the enemy aircraft before taking to his parachute, whilst the stricken German narrowly misses Buckingham Palace and crashes on Victoria Station.

There are various echoes of truth here. On 16 August 1940, Flight Lieutenant James Brindley Nicolson of 249 Squadron was leading his section of Hurricanes over Southampton when they were jumped by enemy fighters, now believed to have been Me 109s. One of Nicolson's pilots, Pilot Officer Martyn Aurel King, the youngest of the Few at eighteen, was shot down and killed, and his No 3, Squadron Leader Eric King, was shot-up and crash-landed. Nicolson was hit and set on fire. As 'Nick' was preparing to bale out, he saw an enemy aircraft in front of him, so climbed back into the furnace-like cockpit and opened fire, before finally exiting his machine.

Badly burned and wounded by a cannon shell, Nicolson was awarded Fighter Command's sole Victoria Cross of the Second World War. Also, on 'Battle of Britain Day', a KG76 Do 17, having been attacked by a host of RAF fighters, was abandoned by the crew and did crash on Victoria Station; the pilot, Oberleutnant Robert Zehbe, landed by parachute at Kennington and was so roughly handled by a civilian mob that he subsequently died. The scene concludes with the charming Pilot Officer Archie landing by parachute on a suburban London greenhouse – the young schoolboy of the house (Steve Morley) immediately fetching and offering the pilot one of his father's cigarettes: 'Thanks awfully, old chap!'

The Big and 'Fantastic' Story: Battle of Britain in Context 207

1:52/2:12   Again, we return to the troubled Harvey marriage, Colin calling from his Scottish base, enquiring whether Maggie, on duty at a bombed-out operations room in 11 Group, has applied for the posting North he so insists upon. Maggie, however, is totally committed and preoccupied, during what is the climax of the Battle of Britain – which is no time for applying for postings to quieter sectors.

1:54/2:12   Although there is no narrative explaining this, Squadron Leader Harvey's 'Dogtail Squadron' then goes South, to relieve a depleted unit, the next scene cutting to another huge Luftwaffe attack – with Harvey in the thick of it. Again, more superb combat footage, in which Harvey gets a 109 but then becomes a 'flamer', only narrowly escaping from his Spitfire before it blows up. After more combat and watching Harvey alight safely by parachute in a cornfield, the scene moves to Section Officer Maggie Harvey and her Corporal, Seymour (Pat Heywood) giving orders to their flight of WAAFs – and Group Captain Baker appearing to give Maggie the news that Colin has been shot down and badly burned, whilst assuring her that 'They can do wonders these days', and, ironically, 'We'll get you a posting, so you can be near him'. Beyond doubt, fire was the fighter pilot's greatest fear, the main fuel tank in a Spitfire and Hurricane being immediately in front of the cockpit, underneath and behind the 109 pilot's seat. And certainly, the brilliant surgeon Archibald McIndoe and his team at East Grinstead Hospital did indeed 'work wonders' of pioneering plastic surgery on their so-called 'Guinea Pigs', those brave, disfigured airmen of whose celebrated number Squadron Leader Harvey would soon be amongst.

1:57/2:12   With Harvey gone, a flight commander takes over the Squadron and 'Peter' is elevated to Red Section Leader, his numbers two and three being 'a couple of new lads', two unidentified, anxious looking and very young, inexperienced, pilot officers: 'Stick to me like glue – and keep your eyes open'. Although usually pilots fresh from Operational Training Unit went to squadrons in quieter sectors, this did not always happen. One example springing readily to mind is nineteen-year-old Pilot Officer Robin Rafter, formerly an army co-operation pilot who answered Fighter Command's call for volunteers.

On 31 August 1940, whereas an experienced and older pilot who converted to Spitfires with Rafter was posted to 13 Group, Rafter arrived at Hornchurch, which was heavily bombed that day, to join 603 Squadron. He would not fly his first operational sortie until 5 September 1940 – when he was almost immediately shot down and wounded in a big engagement with German fighters over Kent.

It was not a case, however, of these inexperienced pilots arriving on a squadron and being expected to jump into a Spitfire and Hurricane and 'get one up'. This was not practical or safe for them or anyone else. Every effort was made to at least give 'sprogs' some local flying experience, even at the busiest sectors, before sending them into battle. This scene, therefore, is a little exaggerated but makes a point well – combat experienced pilots were now in short supply.

1:58/2:12	We move again to the underground operations room at 11 Group's Uxbridge HQ, a scene of great activity as we approach the film's climax. On this day, Churchill visited, inquiring of Air Vice-Marshal Park what reserves there were: he was told 'None'. Certainly, all of 11 Group's squadrons would soon be engaged over London, and those of 12 Group's 'Big Wing' along with other reinforcing squadrons from 10 Group, but this comment should not be interpreted as there being no reserves at all. There were, in 10, 12 and 13 Groups. The next few minutes of aerial footage, supported by Sir William Walton's superb 'Battle in the Air', are so brilliant that they require little comment. By the end of this sequence, with German aircraft falling out of the sky in droves, there is no doubt that the Germans have suffered a major defeat.
2:03/2:12	Across the Channel, the Germans' previously exuberant and over-confident mood of a few weeks previously has given way to depression. Falke dines in silence at a table with his officers – candles burning in the empty places of those killed or missing. By now, it was clear that the Luftwaffe was incapable, in spite of Göring's boastful assurances, of

The Big and 'Fantastic' Story: Battle of Britain in Context 209

	defeating Fighter Command, and the emphasis of their attack now shifted to the night Blitz on cities – implied by a section of He 111s taking off at dusk.
2:04/2:12	In a London tube, sheltering civilians are ecstatic hearing the 9 pm BBC radio news that 165 German aircraft have been destroyed, against thirty fighters lost with ten pilots safe. The British actually claimed 185 destroyed, the true figure being fifty-six, less, in fact, than on 15 August 1940 (seventy-five) and 18 August 1940 (sixty-nine), but clearly the enemy was unable to continue sustaining such heavy losses indefinitely. Fighter Command losses were actually better than represented in this scene: twenty-six fighters lost and eleven pilots killed.

At the time, everyone sensed that this was the turning point, and rightly so. Indeed, this day, 15 September 1940 went down in history as 'Battle of Britain Day'. Interestingly, the radio broadcast concludes by informing listeners that 'Buckingham Palace has again been bombed' – indicating that in this, the 'People's War', everyone was in it together, regardless of rank or status. It was actually to the King and Queen's great credit, in fact, that they remained in London throughout the Battle of Britain and subsequent Blitz, winning much respect from the people.

2:05/2:12	Now back to Dowding's office and a call from the Air Minister, desperate to confirm the claims for the American press, Dowding's attitude being disinterest in propaganda, responding that 'if we are right, they'll give up; if we're wrong, they'll be in London in a week'. Dowding was a pragmatic man with a sound technical mind, not given to politics, which is the point of this scene, in addition to emphasising the importance of proving to neutral America that Britain was successfully holding and far from a lost cause.
2:06/2:12	We are then returned to Rabbit Squadron's base, with pilots, including Pilot Officer Archie and Sergeant-Pilot Andy, disembarking from a truck at dispersal for readiness. The telephone rings, just to say 'tea's up', causing a keyed-up pilot to vomit outside. Here then, is fear, an attempt to make

these fabled knights of the air 'human'. Unusually, given the intense fighting over recent weeks, there is no enemy air activity. Silence descends over the airfields and operations rooms.

Then, we are shown the Germans abandoning invasion preparations, the impression being that the Battle of Britain has been won – and that the daylight fighting simply and abruptly *stopped*. It did not. Indeed, from 20 September 1940 onwards, the Germans began using fighter-bombers in their high-altitude fighter sweeps, meaning that every incursion had to be intercepted by Fighter Command – a period many RAF pilots remembered as the most exhausting and one during which arguably the German fighters, no longer chained to the close escort role, achieved a degree of ascendency. The two fighter forces, in fact, continued to clash by day until February 1941, when bad weather brought a stop to it.

2:09/2:12   By now, the outcome being clear, Göring is incandescent with rage at his Luftwaffe's failure, ranting from his train at Kesselring and Osterkamp about what he sees as a betrayal. As his train pulls away, Osterkamp gives the normal military salute – whilst Kesselring raises his right arm in the Nazi style. This scene had, in fact, infuriated General Galland, causing all kinds of arguments, but the film's producers refused to delete the Nazi salute – and Kesselring was, after all, a Party member. Eventually, when Galland saw the scene he was mollified, as it is a dignified one not treating the Germans as figures of fun - although the General always maintained that the scene was unnecessary. The scene, however, does show a division in the military between Nazis and those simply fighting for Germany. It was not, however, the first time that the Nazi salute was used in the film: at 13:05, when Milch and Jeschonnek are seen entering Hitler's office, both give their Führer the *Hitlergruß* (or Hitler Greeting), as does Baron von Richter at 13:40, when also given an audience with Hitler.

2:10/2:12   The final scene is Dowding's triumph, the battle over, he leaves his office via the terrace, overlooking the formal gardens of Bentley Priory, towards London. Churchill's immortal phrase then appears over a blue sky: 'Never in the field of human conflict has so much been owed by so many to so Few' – leaving us in no doubt whatsoever of the enormity of Fighter Command's achievement. Finally, the casualty statistics indicate the Finest Hour's human cost, nation by nation, demonstrating that it was a broad multi-national force which kept Britain free in 1940. True, neither side was decisively defeated at the end of this sixteen-week conflict – but Hitler's proposed invasion was off, and would never happen. And that, of course, is what the Battle of Britain was all about.

Battle of Britain, then, succeeded in telling the big story, whilst taking some liberties, by necessity with micro detail and concluding with the false impression of an abrupt and final defeat. The aerial scenes are second to none and out-takes remain film-makers standard go-to source for such footage even today. The film was made over fifty years ago now, long before the digital age, and those aerial scenes, using largely real aircraft, are its strength. Today, some talk of a 're-make', which personally I hope never happens – because, for all the modern age's digital wizardry, Computer Generated Images just do not compare to those twisting, turning, iconic, real machines.

Whilst academic historians in particular remain vexed and continue debating the merits or otherwise of history on film, there is an argument that unfaithful though some 'historical' films are to history, they can be of value through igniting interest in the viewer and inspiring a need to know more. All kinds of benefits for the historical record could arise from such a circumstance. Having first watched *Battle of Britain* as an eight-year-old schoolboy upon release in 1969, were that not the case, I would not be writing this…

As Guy Hamilton said, the Battle of Britain is a '*fantastic* story'.

Appendix I

1969 – A Year in Film and Television

The year 1969 produced a mixed bag of entertainment for the large and small screen. At the cinema it was the year that John Wayne won a long-awaited Oscar for his role in *True Grit*, and the final year of the 1960s also saw the passing of two all-time silver screen greats, Robert Taylor and Judy Garland. On the television it was a year of crimefighters and special agents. Sir Lew Grade's ATV organisation was producing such fare as *The Champions*, *Randall and Hopkirk (Deceased)* and *Strange Report*, to name just three. The following listings are but a sampling of what was being aired for our entertainment at the same time as *Battle of Britain*.

Cinema

Anne of a Thousand Days
Butch Cassidy and the Sundance Kid
Cactus Flower
Decline and Fall of a Birdwatcher
Easy Rider
Goodbye, Mr Chips
Gypsy Moths
Hamlet
Hello Dolly
If
Lock Up Your Daughters
Mayerling
Midnight Cowboy
Oh, What a Lovely War
Once Upon A Time in the West
On Her Majesty's Secret Service
Otley
Paint Your Wagon
Play Dirty
Sweet Charity
The Damned
The Italian Job
The Love Bug
The Prime of Miss Jean Brodie
The Royal Hunt of the Sun
The Wild Bunch
Three Into Two Won't Go
True Grit
Where Eagles Dare

1969 – A Year in Film and Television

Television

Big Breadwinner Hog
Cilla
Clangers
Curry and Chips
Dad's Army
Department 'S'
Doctor in the House
Father, Dear Father
Hadleigh
Holiday 69
Joe 90
Magpie
A Man of Our Times
Man on the Moon
Marty
Monty Python's Flying Circus
Nearest and Dearest
On The Buses
Please Sir
Randall and Hopkirk (Deceased)
Special Branch
Stars on Sunday
Strange Report
The Champions
The Dave Allen Show
The Liver Birds
Wheel of Fortune

Appendix II

Battle of Britain 'Stars' Filmography

To many of the major stars, *Battle of Britain* was just another acting role. Some of them spent as little as four days on the film, while others spent as much as four months committing their parts to celluloid. The cast list was indeed an impressive one, with most of the participants having been employed for many years in the movie business. Sadly, as the years pass, less and less of the film's cast remain with us, but nevertheless, all who took part in *Battle* contributed a great deal to British cinema and the impact it had on the rest of the world. The following filmography is not intended to include every film made by the main actors mentioned, but to give a feel for the wide range of material covered by the cast of *Battle of Britain*.

Harry Andrews (1911–1989)
The Red Beret – 1952, A Hill in Korea – 1956, Ice Cold in Alex – 1958, 633 Squadron – 1964, The Charge of the Light Brigade – 1968, Entertaining Mr Sloane – 1970, Death on the Nile – 1978, Superman – 1978, Hawk the Slayer – 1980.

Michael Bates (1920–1978)
I'm All Right Jack – 1959, Bedazzled – 1967, Here We Go Round the Mulberry Bush – 1967, Hammer Head – 1968, Patton – 1970, A Clockwork Orange – 1971, Frenzy – 1972, No Sex Please, We're British – 1973.

Michael Caine (1933 –)
A Hill in Korea – 1956, The Wrong Arm of the Law – 1962, Zulu – 1964, The Ipcress File – 1965, Alfie – 1966, Gambit – 1966, Play Dirty – 1967, The Italian Job – 1969, Get Carter – 1971, Sleuth – 1972, The Eagle Has Landed – 1976, Educating Rita – 1983, The Whistle Blower – 1986, The Fourth Protocol – 1987, A Muppet Christmas Carol – 1992, Little Voice – 1998.

Barry Foster (1931–2002)
Sea of Sand – 1956, The Family Way – 1966, Ryan's Daughter – 1970, Frenzy – 1972, The Wild Geese – 1978, The Whistle Blower – 1986.

Edward Fox (1937 –)
The Naked Runner – 1967, The Go-Between – 1971, Day of the Jackal – 1973, A Bridge Too Far – 1977, Force Ten From Navarone – 1978, Gandhi – 1982, Never Say Never Again – 1983, The Bounty – 1984, Robin Hood – 1990.

Trevor Howard (1913–1988)
The Way Ahead – 1944, The Way to the Stars – 1945, Brief Encounter – 1946, The Third Man – 1949, Odette – 1950, Cockleshell Heroes – 1955, Around the World in 80 Days – 1956, Mutiny on the Bounty – 1962, Von Ryan's Express – 1965, Operation Crossbow – 1965, Ryan's Daughter – 1970, Kidnapped – 1972, Aces High –1976, Superman – 1978, The Sea Wolves – 1980.

Curt Jurgens (1915–1982)
Me and the Colonel – 1957, The Enemy Below – 1957, Inn of the Sixth Happiness – 1958, Ferry to Hong Kong – 1958, Lord Jim – 1964, The Assassination Bureau – 1968, Soft Beds and Hard Battles – 1974, The Spy Who Loved Me – 1977.

Ian McShane (1942 –)
Sky West and Crooked – 1966, Villain – 1971, Ransom – 1974, Dirty Money – 1979, Sexy Beast – 2000, Pirates of the Caribbean: On Stranger Tides – 2011, Jack The Giant Slayer – 2013, Cuban Fury – 2014, Hellboy – 2019.

Kenneth More (1914–1982)
Scott of the Antarctic – 1948, Chance of a Lifetime – 1950, No Highway – 1951, Genevieve – 1953, Reach for the Sky – 1956, The Admirable Crichton – 1957, A Night to Remember – 1958, The Thirty Nine Steps – 1959, Sink the Bismarck – 1960, The Longest Day – 1962, Scrooge – 1970, The Spaceman and King Arthur – 1979.

Sir Laurence Olivier (1907–1989)
Too Many Crooks – 1930, Perfect Understanding – 1932, Conquest of the Air – 1935, Q Planes – 1939, Rebecca – 1940, 49th Parallel – 1941,

Henry V – 1944, Hamlet – 1948, The Magic Box – 1951, Richard III – 1956, Spartacus – 1960, The Entertainer – 1960, Shoes of the Fisherman – 1968, Lady Caroline Lamb – 1972, Sleuth – 1972, A Bridge Too Far – 1977, The Boys From Brazil – 1978, Dracula – 1979, Clash of the Titans – 1981, The Jazz Singer – 1981, The Bounty – 1984, Lost Empires – 1986.

Christopher Plummer (1927 –2021)
Stage Struck – 1958, Fall of the Roman Empire – 1964, The Sound of Music – 1965, The Night of the Generals – 1967, Triple Cross – 1967, The Royal Hunt of the Sun – 1969, Waterloo – 1970, The Spiral Staircase – 1975, The Man Who Would Be King – 1975, The Return of the Pink Panther – 1975, Aces High – 1976, Hanover Street – 1979, Dragnet – 1987, Star Trek VI – 1991. All The Money in the World – 2017.

Sir Ralph Richardson (1902–1983)
The Ghoul – 1933, Things to Come – 1936, Thunder in the City – 1937, Q Planes – 1939, The Lion Has Wings – 1939, School for Secrets – 1946, Outcast of the Islands – 1951, The Sound Barrier – 1952, Exodus – 1961, Doctor Zhivago – 1966, The Wrong Box – 1966, Oh What a Lovely War – 1969, David Copperfield – 1969, A Doll's House – 1973, Time Bandits – 1980, Dragonslayer – 1981.

Robert Shaw (1927–1978)
The Dambusters – 1955, A Hill in Korea – 1956, From Russia With Love – 1963, The Battle of the Bulge – 1965, A Man for all Seasons – 1966, Custer of the West – 1967, Young Winston – 1972, The Sting – 1973, Jaws – 1975, Robin and Marian – 1975, The Deep – 1977, Force Ten from Navarone – 1978.

Susannah York (1939–2011)
Tunes of Glory – 1960, There Was a Crooked Man – 1960, Tom Jones – 1963, Sands of the Kalahari – 1965, A Man for all Seasons – 1966, The Killing of Sister George – 1968, Country Dance – 1970, Gold – 1974, Conduct Unbecoming – 1975, Superman – 1978, Yellowbeard – 1983, A Summer Story – 1988, Pretty Princess – 1993.

Appendix III

Also Seen In …

Since 1969, several films and television programmes have used outtakes, offcuts, call them what you will, from *Battle of Britain*, and this, including footage never seen before, still crops up from time to time, over 50 years after the movie was premiered.

1971	*Dad's Army*; film spin off from the popular television series
1972	*The Pathfinders*; ITV television drama series based on the exploits of Bomber Command's Pathfinder Force
1972	*Our Miss Fred*; a film comedy starring Danny la Rue
1976	*Carry on England*; a film from the long running *Carry On* series
1976	*Battle of Midway*; a war film dramatising the Japanese attack on Midway Island in 1942
1979	*Breakthrough* (aka *Sergeant Steiner*); a war film starring Richard Burton
1984	*The Secret War of Jackie's Girls*; a television movie
1986	*Murrow*; a Channel 4 television drama based on the life of Ed Murrow, wartime news correspondent
1988	*A Piece of Cake*; a television drama series based around an RAF fighter squadron in 1940
1999	*Finest Hour*; a BBC Television documentary series chronicling the events of 1940
2001	*Dark Blue World*; a feature film about Czech pilots flying in the Battle of Britain
2005	*Fighting The Blue*; a documentary series covering the Battle of Britain using extensive outtakes from the film
2010	*First Light*; the drama/documentary recalling the wartime experiences of Battle of Britain Spitfire pilot Squadron Leader Geoffrey Wellum DFC, and based upon his book of the same name

Acknowledgements

Robert Rudhall, for the Original Edition

This book has been a veritable labour of love and I have been helped along the way by a whole host of friends, colleagues and acquaintances, who have not only put up with my obsession for the *Battle of Britain* film, but come to my aid on many occasions, be it with information, photographs, or words of advice and encouragement. To you all I offer my sincere thanks. If there is anyone who has inadvertently been missed off the following list, I apologise and I will endeavour to rectify the omissions if a second edition of this book should ever see the light of day.

 Peter R. Arnold, for his knowledge and expertise on Spitfires along with many other aspects of the film's production; Derek Baker, for sparing the time to be interviewed between film assignments; Vivian Bellamy, for his recollections of flying in the film; John Blake, for his time spent remembering his involvement in the film; Roy Bonser, for the loan of photographs; Patrick Boone, for the loan of photographs; British Film Institute stills department staff, for their friendly co-operation during several visits to source photographs; Gary R. Brown, for his enthusiasm for the project, research on the surviving aircraft and loan of photographs; Chris Chandler, for the use of photographs; Tony Clarke, for the use of photographs; Classic FM radio station, for keeping me company during the long hours of writing of this book; Colin Cooper, for the loan of photographs; Frank Crosby, the Imperial War Museum Duxford's Press Officer, for lighting the blue touchpaper; Duncan Cubitt, for his guidance and help with the photographic studio work; John Dabbs, for the loan of photographs; Squadron Leader Paul Day OBE AFC Officer Commanding RAF Battle of Britain Memorial Flight, for unhesitatingly agreeing to write the foreword; R.A. Edwards, for the use of photographs; Peter Edwards, for the loan of photographs; Ken Ellis, for his support, very welcome advice and loan of photographs; John S. Fairey, for supplying the Spitfire Mk.68

Acknowledgements 219

Pilots Notes; Steve Fletcher, for photo studio work; Ron Goodwin, for his friendship and detailed recall of composing the film's music; Anja Hadfield of the Press Association for help in sourcing photographs; Mark Hanna, for convincing me that I should go ahead and write this book; J. Holder, for loan of photographs; Frederic Lert, for use of photographs; Donald MaCarron, for the use of photographs; T.G. 'Hamish' Mahaddie, for his friendship during the final ten years of his life and for the supply of film documents etc; Peter R. March, for the supply of photographs; Tony Overill, for the loan of photographs; Chris Pointon, for the use of his photographs; Francois Prins, for his encouragement, knowledge of the film and loan of photographs; Steve Reglar, for the loan of photographs; Steve Rickards, for his research into, and unlimited enthusiasm for the film; Paul Robinson, for help in compiling the cast and credits list; Peter Sargent, for the use and donation of his extensive photo archive; Dilip and Anita Sarkar, for making my dream come true and publishing this book; Mike Springett, for his supply of photographs; the staff at Stamford Photo Express for their highly professional service; D. Thatcher, for the loan of photographs; and last but by no means least, Mike Vickers, for his many memories of flying Spitfires, Hurricanes and Messerschmitts in the film.

Plus: Mark Ansell, John Ashby, Adrian Balch, Paul Barber, Sue Blunt, P.H. Brook, Alan Browne, J.M. Butt, D.M. Cobb, Martin Collins, A.J. Datson, Brian Dorer, Paul Doyle, Paul Dunkerley, A. Fanning, A.G. Fennell, David Griffith, J.P. Griffin, T. Hale, A. Hextall, P. Holmes, Doug Jones, Terence Kelly, James Kightly, Andrew Mahaddie, Peter J. Marson, Ken Playfoot, Arthur J. Pullin, Graham Quinn, Don Ream, W.G. Richards, R.J. Robinson, Lee Roblett, Mike Sheahan, Jim Shields, Christine Swettenham, Ray Thomas, Malcolm T. Walls, G. Weight, Roy Williams, Paul Welch, G. Wells, Ken Wortelhock.

Dilip Sarkar, for the New Edition
It has been both a pleasure and privilege to oversee the collaboration necessary to produce this updated volume; the updates provided by Gary Brown, Peter Arnold and Paul Robinson have been essential and Joyce, Robert's widow, and I are extremely grateful to all for that input. I also thank Mrs Julia Williams for permission to quote from the memoirs of her late father, Wg Cdr R.G. Kellett DSO, DFC, VM. As always, Martin Mace and the Pen & Sword team have been a pleasure to work with.

Bibliography

Original Edition

Many different sources have been referred to during the writing of this book, all of which can be recommended for further information regarding the film *Battle of Britain*.

Blokker, Kees, *Ron Goodwin – His Kind of Music* (K. Blokker 1996)
Blum, Daniel, *A Pictorial History of the Talkies* (Hamlyn Publishing 1974)
Bowyer, Chaz, *Bomber Barons* (William Kimber & Co Ltd 1983)
Bowyer, Michael J.F., *The Spitfire 50 Years On* (Patrick Stephens Ltd 1986)
Caiden, Martin, *Me 109* (Macdonald & Co 1969)
Chapman, John, and Goodall, Geoff, *Warbirds Directory* (Warbirds Media Company 1996)
Cinebooks, *Virgin Film Guide – Sixth Edition* (Virgin Books 1997)
Coulson, Ray C., *Spitfire – A Look Back Over the Gate* (R.C. Coulson 1994)
Ellis, Ken, and Butler, Phil, *British Museum Aircraft* (Merseyside Aviation Society 1977)
Ellis, Ken, *In Uniform* (Merseyside Aviation Society 1983)
Ellis, Ken, *Wrecks and Relics 16th Edition* (Midland Publishing Ltd 1998)
Farmer, James, *Broken Wings* (Pictorial Histories Publishing Company 1984)
Farmer, James, *Celluloid Wings* (Tab Books Inc 1984)
Freeman, Roger, *Airfields of the Eighth – Then and Now* (Battle of Britain Prints International Ltd 1978)
Gilbert, James, *The Great Planes* (Hamlyn Publishing 1970)
Hutchinson, Tom, *Battle of Britain – from the Great New Motion Picture* (Purnell 1969)
Jeavons, Clyde, *A Pictorial History of War Films* (Hamlyn Publishing 1974)
Jones, David, *Film Fanatics Guide* (Merlin Books Ltd 1988)
Mahaddie, T.G., *Hamish - the Story of a Pathfinder* (Ian Allan Ltd 1989)
Mosley, Leonard, *The Battle of Britain – the making of a film* (Weidenfeld and Nicolson, 1969)
Paris, Michael, *From the Wright Brothers to Top Gun* (Manchester University Press 1995)
Peel, Dave, *British Civil Aircraft Registers Since 1919* (Midland Counties Publications 1985)
Pendo, Stephen, *Aviation in the Cinema* (Scarecrow Press 1985)

Ramsey, Winston G., *The Battle of Britain – Then and Now* (Battle of Britain Prints International Ltd 1980)
Riley, Gordon, and Trant, Graham, *Spitfire Survivors* (Aston Publications 1986)
Sarkar, Dilip, *Bader's Duxford Fighters – The Big Wing Controversy* (Ramrod Publications 1997)
Simpson, Jim, *RAF Gate Guards* (Airlife Publishing 1992)
Skogsberg, Bertil, *Wings on the Silver Screen* (Tantivy Press 1979)
Taylor, Bill, *The Battle of Britain Memorial Flight* (Midland Publishing Ltd 1995)
Thompson, Scott, *B-25 Mitchell in Civil Service* (Aero Vintage Books 1997)
Van der Kooij, *European Wrecks and Relics Vol 2* (Midland Publishing Ltd 1998)
Walker, John, *Halliwell's Film & Video Guide 2000* (Harper Collins 1999)
Walker, John, *Halliwell's Who's Who in the Movies* (Harper Collins 1999)
Winnert, Derek, *Radio Times Film and Video Guide* (Hodder & Stoughton 1993)
Wood, Derek with Dempster, Derek, *The Narrow Margin* (Arrow Books 1969)

Plus the following periodicals: *After the Battle No 1* 1973; *Aircraft Illustrated Extra* August 1969; *Airfix Magazine* February 1969; *Air Pictorial* September 1969; *Control Column* Vol 2 No 5, Vol 2 No 6, Vol 3 No 10, Vol 5 No 10; *EAA Warbirds* July 1992; *Flight International* September 1969; *FlyPast* September 1989, October 1989, September 1999; *Scale Models* October 1969; *Warbirds Worldwide* 7, 8, 9 & 47. Use was also made of information contained in Derek Coyte's 'Briefings', a series of publications issued from Pinewood Film Studios to theatre managers all over the world, prior to *Battle of Britain*'s release on the cinema circuit.

For Reel 15 in the New Edition
Films:
Battle of Britain, Directed by Guy Hamilton, Spitfire Productions, Pinewood Studios, London, 1969
Angels One Five, Directed by George More O'Ferrell, Templar, Pinewood Studios, London, 1952
Reach for the Sky, Directed by Lewis Gilbert, Rank Organisation, Pinewood Studios, London, 1956
The One That Got Away, Directed by Roy Ward Baker, Julian Wintle Productions, Pinewood Studios, London, 1957

Unpublished Sources:
Kellett, Wg Cdr R.G., Memoirs, 1978

The National Archives:
AIR27/1663, 303 Squadron Operations Record Book
AIR50/117/45, Fg Off L Paskiewicz Combat Report, 30 August 1940

Published Sources:
Addison, P., & Crang, J.A., (Eds), *The Burning Blue: A New History of the Battle of Britain*, Pimlico, London, 2000
Anon (Polish Air Force Association in Great Britain), *Destiny Can Wait: The Polish Air Force in the Second World War*, William Heinemann Ltd, London, 1949
Calder, A., *The Myth of the Blitz*, |Pimlico, London, 2008
Clapson, M., *The Routledge Companion to Britain in the Twentieth Century*, Routledg, Abingdon, 2009
Foreman, J., *RAF Fighter Command Victory Claims of World War Two, Part One 1939-1940*, Red Kite, Walton-on-Thames, 2003
Franks, N.L.R., *RAF Fighter Command Losses of the Second World War, Volume 1, Operational Losses: Aircraft and Crews, 1939-41*, Midland, Hersham, 2008
Galland, General A., *The First and the Last*, Cerberus Publishing, Bristol, 2001
Kent, Wg Cdr J., *One of the Few*, History Press, Stroud, 2008
MacKenzie, S.P., *The Battle of Britain on Screen: "The Few" in British Film and Television Drama*, Edinburgh University Press, Edinburgh, 2007
Mosley, L., *Battle of Britain*, Pan Books, London, 1969
Overy, R., *The Battle*, Penguin, London, 2000
Ponting, C., *1940: Myth & Reality*, Hamish Hamilton Ltd, London, 1990
Ramsey, W. (Ed), *The Blitz Then & Now: Volume 1*, Battle of Britain Prints International Ltd, London, 1987
Sarkar, D., *The Few: The Battle of Britain in the Words of the Pilots*, Amberley Publishing, Stroud, 2009
——, *The Bader Wings: The Duxford Wings Controversy*, Pen & Sword Ltd, Barnsley, 2021
——, *'Sailor' Malan: Freedom Fighter, the Inspirational Story of a Fighter Ace*, Pen & Sword Ltd, Barnsley, 2021
Smith, M., *Britain & 1940: History, Myth & Popular Memory*, Routledge, London, 2000